Working from a place of rest

Text copyright © Tony Horsfall 2010
The author asserts the moral right
to be identified as the author of this work

Published by
The Bible Reading Fellowship
15 The Chambers, Vineyard
Abingdon OX14 3FE
United Kingdom
Tel: +44 (0)1865 319700
Email: enquiries@brf.org.uk
Website: www.brf.org.uk
BRF is a Registered Charity

ISBN 978 1 84101 544 6

First published 2010
Reprinted twice 2011
10 9 8 7 6 5 4 3 2
All rights reserved

Acknowledgments
Unless otherwise stated, scripture quotations are taken from the Holy Bible, New International
Version, copyright © 1973, 1978, 1984 by International Bible Society, are used by permission
of Hodder & Stoughton Publishers, a member of the Hachette Livre UK Group. All rights
reserved. 'NIV' is a registered trademark of International Bible Society. UK trademark number
1448790.

The Living Bible copyright © Tyndale House Publishers 1971. All rights reserved.

Scripture quotations from THE MESSAGE. Copyright © Eugene H. Peterson 1993, 1994, 1995.
Used by permission of NavPress Publishing.

Extracts from the Authorised Version of the Bible (The King James Bible), the rights in which
are vested in the Crown, are reproduced by permission of the Crown's Patentee, Cambridge
University Press.

The paper used in the production of this publication was supplied by mills that source their
raw materials from sustainably managed forests. Soy-based inks were used in its printing and
the laminate film is biodegradable.

A catalogue record for this book is available from the British Library

Printed in Singapore by Craft Print International Ltd

Working from a place of rest

Jesus and the key to sustaining ministry

Tony Horsfall

This book is dedicated to...
all those men and women throughout the world whose lives are given to serving God, especially those who work in cross-cultural situations, and in particular the staff of Mission Aviation Fellowship International (Africa Region), who have a special place in my heart.
May you be encouraged and sustained in your calling.

Contents

It's important to drink and be refreshed on the journey

It's humbling to see God at work on the journey

❖

Foreword

'How are you?'

'Fine' used to be the standard response to that question. These days, 'busy' seems to be the socially approved reply. We respect busy people and we want people to know that we are busy. Bumper stickers proclaim, 'Jesus is coming—look busy'. Christians proudly sing, 'We will give ourselves no rest'.

My work involves supporting missionaries. The problems I come across most frequently are having too much to do, burn-out and exhaustion. The needs are so great and there are too few workers. I have asked mission personnel ministering in war zones to tell me the main cause of their stress, expecting the answer to be related to war. Instead, 'heavy workload' has been reported as the key cause of stress.

I can relate to people who feel busy. I am blessed by having a young child to care for. I receive urgent emails about difficult situations around the world. I have teaching to prepare, resources to write, deadlines to meet, people to see, meetings to attend and much more. It is not surprising that I rarely manage to finish reading a book.

This book is the exception. I finished it within three days. Much more importantly, it has changed my thinking and my behaviour.

Tony Horsfall has brought principles about rest home to me in a new way, and has given practical suggestions which are helping me to put into practice what I believe. Tony is already the author I recommend most often as I teach and try to help others. This book brings new insights into what we mean by rest, and why and how to achieve it.

How liberating it is to realise that Jesus rested, said 'no' to demands and allowed needs to go unmet! This book can help us discern what God wants us to say 'yes' to, and when to say 'no'; it can help us learn to build margin into our lives so that we work from a place of rest.

How are you? Busy? If so, and especially if you do not have time to read books, then this is the book for you.

Dr Debbie Hawker, InterHealth

✤

Introduction

One of the amazing things about the Bible is that you can be reading a familiar passage and suddenly the words seem to leap off the page and hit you between the eyes. All at once the significance of what you are reading bursts unexpectedly into your consciousness, and you become aware that God is speaking to you in a profound way.

It is rather like one of those grand firework displays. There is a bang, a burst of light, and coloured stars begin shooting in all directions. *Then* another, and another, until the whole sky is lit up. All you can do is stand back and watch in amazement. So it is with these moments of revelation, of spiritual illumination, of knowing something you never knew before. Your eyes are opened to a truth that was previously hidden; that which was obscure becomes plain; and it is not something you are making happen. It is the work of the Holy Spirit, taking the truth of God and making it known to you through the words of scripture. As one truth dawns, another opens up before you in the incredible unfolding process of spiritual awareness.

I enjoyed one such moment some years ago when I was reading through John chapter 4. I came to the passage in the course of a reading scheme I was following at the time, and I arrived there with little expectation, having read the story of the woman at the well many times before. I was not expecting to receive anything new, merely to be reminded of familiar truths. Then I came to verse 6, and the fireworks began: 'Jacob's well was there, and Jesus, tired as he was from the journey, sat down by the well. It was about the sixth hour.'

In a flash I saw the tremendous significance of these simple words and realised something quite staggering in its implications. *Jesus was doing nothing.* He was having a rest, taking a break, giving himself a breather. Sitting there on the edge of the well, he was pausing and giving himself permission to stop and simply to be.

Then, just as quickly, the thought came to me that *everything that happens in this story happens because Jesus was doing nothing.* The fact that he is resting, taking some time out, is what gives him the opportunity to 'waste' time with the Samaritan woman who comes to the well while he is sitting there. Because of that life-giving conversation, not only is her life changed but the whole Samaritan town experiences revival. None of this is premeditated or planned. It is a purely spontaneous event, dependent on the fact that Jesus is doing nothing.

While I was still trying to get my head around this second insight, a third suddenly arrived. *We can learn to work and minister as Jesus did, from a place of rest.* Christian ministry need not be a matter of striving to make things happen or of straining to achieve our goals through the sweat of our brow. We can learn to work together with God just as Jesus did, for this was no idle moment; rather, it was a moment of communion, of sensing what the Father was doing and of responding accordingly. We can learn to co-labour with God, to collaborate with his Spirit and work in a way that is both efficient and effective. The work is not ours; it is his. If we slow down and take time to listen, he will guide us so that we can share in what he is doing. We can learn to live, to work and to minister to others from a place of resting in God.

I continued to ponder this verse over the next few weeks and months, and to develop my thoughts around the five headings you will find in this book. I have road-tested the material many times in seminars and retreats, and there has always been a good response. People seem to recognise this as something they already knew deep down inside but perhaps did not dare articulate. I continue to read around the subject to gain a broader understanding and I am continually reflecting on my own experience in the light of what I am sharing here, to see if it really does work. I think it does. I offer my thoughts to you with the prayer that they may liberate you into a healthier and more fruitful way of serving God.

The Evangelical Alliance (an umbrella organisation for many churches and organisations in the United Kingdom) met in September 2008 to address what it called a 'crisis in leadership' in the church in Britain. As well as an ageing leadership and a lack of emerging younger leaders, it noted that there is a depletion of leaders, because many drop out through exhaustion and depression.

This certainly concurs with my own observations. It is my privilege to work with church leaders, missionaries and key lay people in different parts of the world. 'Exhaustion' is a common word used, and 'tiredness' a number one problem for many. 'Burnout' is something we are familiar with as a potential threat and, for some, a personal reality. I do not claim to have all the answers and I still struggle myself in some of these areas, but I believe that learning to work and minister in the way that Jesus did must be part of the answer.

So come and sit by the well for a while. Take some time out to reflect on how you are living and working. Watch Jesus and see how he does it. Listen to what the Spirit may be saying to you deep within, at the centre of your being; and maybe, just maybe, God will give you some insights that will change your life and sustain your ministry over the long haul.

It's helpful to think of life
as a journey

1

Jesus on a journey

The context of the story we are looking at in John 4:1–43 is found in Jesus' decision to leave Judea and return to Galilee. It appears that, in this early part of his public ministry, he is being particularly effective and that many new disciples are being baptised. News of this has reached the Pharisees and, aware of a potential backlash from these religious conservatives, Jesus makes a strategic decision to return to his homeland in the north. The time will come when he clashes head-on with these powerful religious figures but this is not the time for confrontation. Rather, he chooses to withdraw to the quieter shores of Galilee, away from the spotlight, to where his fledgling group of disciples can be nurtured without too much negative attention.

So we find Jesus on the road again, as we so often see him in the Gospels. Walking with his disciples, crisscrossing the countryside from place to place, provided him with many natural opportunities for developing friendship with them, for informal teaching and for sharing life together. I'm sure he enjoyed these journeys and the camaraderie that grew between them as they travelled.

This particular journey was problematic for any devout and conscientious Jew, however. The easiest and quickest route was to pass through Samaria, but that might mean having to make contact with people whom they despised. The Samaritans were descended from Jews who had not been deported during the time of the Assyrian exile, but had intermarried with foreigners and adopted a syncretistic form of worship. They were considered by devout Jews to be a mixed race, and religiously impure. The hostility was mutual and Jewish travellers were not always welcomed in Samaritan villages. Consequently, most Jewish travellers chose to take a longer route, which meant crossing the River Jordan in order to bypass Samaria, and only crossing back when they were safely beyond Samaritan presence.

What is surprising on this journey is that Jesus deliberately chooses to travel through Samaria. 'Now he *had to* go through Samaria,' writes John (4:4, italics mine), using a word that suggests a strong sense of necessity. We shall return to the significance of this later, simply noting at this point that his decision would have caused consternation and apprehension among his disciples, but they trust his judgment and the journey begins. Probably early in the morning, just as the sun rises, they take to the road, hoping to make as much progress as possible while the day is cool. By midday they have reached the Samaritan village of Sychar and stop to rest by the well. After some discussion, the disciples head off into the village to buy food while Jesus remains at the well.

This, then, is the background to the journey that Jesus is making in John 4. However, we know that John is the most intuitive of the Gospel writers, and every word he uses seems to be filled with deeper significance. I think we are justified, therefore, in seeing beyond the physical journey that Jesus was making into the spiritual journey in which he was also engaged—the journey that brought him to earth, would take him to the cross, and would climax eventually in his resurrection and his triumphant return to heaven itself.

Theologian Anselm Grun speaks of Jesus as the 'divine traveller'. 'He comes down from heaven to travel with us human beings and time and again to be our guest,' he writes.[1] It reminds us of the journey of incarnation with which John begins his Gospel. 'The Word became flesh,' he says, 'and made his dwelling among us' (1:14). This theme is a constant backdrop to the events that John records and the mystery that the opponents of Jesus could not understand—who he was and where he was from. Jesus himself, however, was never in doubt about his origin, his mission and his eventual destination.

He was aware that he had come down from heaven to bring light into the world (John 3:13, 19) and to bear witness to the truth (18:37). He was conscious that he had been sent by God (8:42) to do his will (6:38), and not to condemn the world but to save it (3:17). This would mean laying down his life, which is why he declared himself to be the bread of life. 'For the bread of God is he who comes down from heaven,' he said, 'and gives life to the world' (6:33). Thus the journey would inevitably lead to suffering and to the cross. He had only a short time to accomplish the Father's will (7:33) before the path of obedience would lead him heavenwards again (13:1, 3). Thus we see him preparing his disciples for his departure with the heartbreaking words, 'I am going away' (see 8:21; 14:28).

The bigger journey that Jesus was making is best summed up in his own words to the disciples in the upper room: 'I came from the Father and entered the world; now I am leaving the world and going back to the Father' (16:28). This is the journey that Jesus made for our salvation, and it is helpful to ponder its sacrificial nature as we glimpse him sitting by the well, pausing for a brief respite on the way. Henri Nouwen has aptly called it 'the descending way of Jesus', a downward direction that he chose over and over again as he followed the Father's will: 'God has descended to us human beings to become a human being with us; and once among us, descended to the total dereliction of one condemned to death.'[2]

Such a journey stands in sharp contrast to the approach of most of us. We desire to be 'upwardly mobile', to climb the ladder of success, get on in the world and find recognition and fame. Even Christian ministry can be seen in these terms—moving from a small church to a larger one, working our way to the top of the organisation, creating a name for ourselves, growing in influence and reputation. Not many want to bury themselves in the hard places of the world where there is little outward success and few know or even care what we do. Yet we are called to have the same attitude of mind that Jesus had, which the apostle Paul so wonderfully describes for us in Philippians 2:5–11.

This passage seems to have been an early Christian hymn, perhaps the first Christmas carol, and it vividly portrays the true nature of the journey that brought Jesus to the well at Sychar that day. Whether or not it was composed by Paul himself is unclear, but it sums up accurately his own understanding of the downward way of Jesus. We can see it in verses 6–8 as a journey of seven descending steps.

- Step 1, 'Who, being in very nature God…': The journey begins in heaven where, as God the Son, Jesus shares equality with God the Father and God the Holy Spirit. Here he is worshipped and adored, sharing the glory of heaven and possessing all the attributes of God, such as omnipotence, omniscience and omnipresence.
- Step 2, '… did not consider equality with God something to be grasped, but made himself nothing…': The journey gets underway as he willingly divests himself of his heavenly glory, choosing to lay aside some of his divine prerogatives and privileges. Theologians are divided as to the extent of the self-emptying that took place, but clearly it involved a significant and costly letting go of what was his by right.
- Step 3, '… taking the very nature of a servant…': Here we see how Jesus steps into the role that the Father has assigned for him as the true Servant of the Lord, predicted by the prophets, such as Isaiah in the Servant Songs (Isaiah 42:1–9; 49:1–6; 50:4–9; 52:13—53:12). He willingly adopts the disposition of a servant, choosing the Father's will before his own and entering our world 'not… to be served, but to serve, and to give his life as a ransom for many' (Mark 10:45).

- Step 4, '… being made in human likeness': Now we reach the deepest mystery of the incarnation and the virgin birth—how it is that God could become a man. What we do know is that the divine life is 'contracted to a span' (to use Charles Wesley's telling phrase) in the womb of Mary, so that when the child is born he is both fully human and divine, able to bear the name Immanuel, meaning 'God with us'.

- Step 5, 'And being found in appearance as a man, he humbled himself…': Having become one of us, the Son of God is now subject to all the laws of human growth and development. The omnipotent one becomes a helpless baby, dependent on others for survival. The omniscient one must learn how to talk, how to count, how to write. The omnipresent one must learn to walk and is limited in time and space, travelling on foot from place to place like the rest of humankind. He is a Jew like other Jews, known and recognised by his name (Jesus), his place of birth (of Nazareth), and his father's occupation (the carpenter's son). This is the point at which we meet him at Jacob's well.

- Step 6, '… and became obedient to death…': Hidden away in the backwater that was Nazareth for most of his life, Jesus eventually begins his public ministry, but always with a single aim in mind—to do the Father's will. Obedience is at the heart of his servanthood and there are no limits to his compliance. He knows that the journey will take him to the cross, so when the time comes he sets his face towards Jerusalem with a steely determination that frightens those around him (Mark 10:32–34). No one will take his life from him; he will lay it down of his own volition, because this is the charge given to him by the Father (John 10:17–18).

- Step 7, '…even death on a cross!': There are many ways to die but the path of obedience takes Jesus to a shameful and agonising death, in which he experiences the rejection, hatred and hostility of his enemies, as well as the wrath of God, as he embraces to himself the just punishment for the sins of the whole world. The journey will take him to the grave, but this lowest point will be the triumphant turning point. Having faithfully dealt with sin and conquered Satan, he can now return victoriously to heaven, his journey over: 'Therefore God exalted him to the highest place and gave him the name that is above every name, that at the name of Jesus every knee should bow, in heaven and on earth and under the earth, and every tongue confess that Jesus Christ is Lord, to the glory of God the Father' (vv. 9–11).

As we consider the journey Jesus made, we can only respond with love and gratitude that he was willing to go to such lengths to save us. Like the shepherd who goes out over the mountains in the dark of night to find the one sheep that is missing, he gladly set out on this most amazing journey of all, that he might find each one of us and bring us back to the Father.

As we watch him sitting by the well, having a well-deserved rest, we see beyond the immediate strain of the journey from Judea to Galilee. We gaze upon one who has left the glories of heaven and, in a few short years, will be on his way to a despised and lonely death at Calvary. And our hearts are filled with adoration, for we know that he walks this path of obedience for our sakes, so that we may have eternal life.

2

The journey we are on

One thing that intrigues me about John 4 is that we are able to pinpoint exactly where Jesus was at a particular moment in time, and what he was doing. Travelling from Judea northwards to Galilee, he has reached the little Samaritan town of Sychar and, finding Jacob's well, he is now resting there after the morning's journey—probably sitting on the edge of the well or leaning against it in the shade. It is midday (the Jewish sixth hour) and the sun is at its hottest. Even a GPS device could hardly have given us a more accurate positioning!

On any journey it is helpful to know where we are at a given moment. Many large cities have map boards strategically placed to help visitors find their way. Such maps usually have a red arrow pointing to a particular spot that says 'YOU ARE HERE'. If we don't know where we are to begin with, it is difficult to know where we should go next. That is why it is always helpful to stop and find our bearings.

The metaphor of the journey is now a well-accepted one for the Christian life. It suggests to us movement, progress and change. It reminds us that we have not arrived but are still in progress, and that Christianity is not a static affair but a dynamic, evolving relationship with a living God. Just as Jesus was on a journey, so we find ourselves on a journey, and at any moment it is helpful to know exactly where we are on that journey. Sometimes the journey will be hard and demanding and we too will need to stop and rest.

I like to think that the journey we are making is composed of three different strands, each in some ways separate and independent but intertwined with the others to make a complete whole. We are called to follow Jesus, and this is the discipleship journey of obedience and faith, which impinges directly on our outward life. Then there is the transformational journey, for we are also called to follow in the footsteps of Jesus and become like him in our character and behaviour. This impinges on our inner life. Finally there is the journey through life, our progression from the cradle to the grave, which impinges on both our outward life and our inner life at different times and in different ways. It provides the context for the other two aspects of the journey.

As we learn to work from a place of rest, it is important that we are familiar with these different strands of the journey, and that we can identify as accurately as possible where we are in each dimension of the journey at any given time. Only then can we become aware of how tiring certain phases of the journey can be, and of why we need to build into our lives opportunity for rest and refreshment. We will need to find our own equivalent of Jacob's well and not be afraid to rest for a while.

Let's think first about the discipleship journey. When Jesus gathered around him the initial group of twelve, he did so with the words 'Come, follow me' (Mark 1:17), and these are still the words of invitation that he speaks to us today. We are called to become his disciples, to accept him as our Teacher, Lord and Master, and so to integrate his will and his teaching into our lives. Jesus was careful to explain the terms of discipleship clearly, not relegating anything to the fine print but openly declaring that if we choose to follow him, he must come first in our lives (8:34–38). The badge of discipleship is the cross, and the cross speaks of self-denial. Furthermore, the Church exists to fulfil what is called the 'great commission' (see Matthew 28:18–20): it requires that we who are disciples should be willing to go out into the world and make other disciples. Christian discipleship can never be a part-time, half-hearted affair. It demands the offering of our lives to God. This is why it is good to stop and look and to see Jesus on the journey he made, for his self-giving love is the motivation and dynamic of our own call to service.

Anyone who takes seriously the words of Jesus must therefore ask the question, 'Lord, what is it you want me to do with my life?' Jesus said, 'As the Father has sent me, I am sending you' (John 20:21) and his coming into the world is the pattern for our own going out into the world. Many will be called to serve him in ordinary professions or in the marketplace, using their skills and abilities for his glory in the realms of education, business, health care and so on. Some will be called to focus in a more specialised way on specific forms of Christian ministry, whether in their own culture or working across cultures to reach different people groups. Neither calling is superior to the other, for both are equally valid and require the same degree of devotion and application.

What is important is that, whatever our calling, we are continually renewed in the midst of that calling. Eugene Peterson has described Christian discipleship as 'a long obedience in the same direction'.[3] Because Christian ministry is demanding and draining, we must have moments of rest when we remind ourselves why we are doing what we are doing, and allow the Lord to call us again to the task or direct us to some other expression of ministry.

It is my privilege to serve as Pastoral Carer for Mission Aviation Fellowship International in their Africa region. This means that I visit their teams in various countries once a year to see how they are doing and to provide spiritual input and care for them. As the name suggests, the purpose of MAF-I is to fly light aircraft in developing countries so that people in remote areas can receive the help they need. The staff is made up of pilots, engineers, avionic technicians and logistical and back-up staff, together with their families.

I have recently returned from a visit to the team in N'djamena, the capital of Chad. This is one of the poorest countries in Africa, and most of it is desert. There are no tourists here and nothing at all appealing about the place. It's very hot and very dusty. Three times in recent years there have been attempted coups, when the staff members have been evacuated at short notice, leaving everything behind. The small team of four families has recently regrouped after the evacuation of February 2008. Life for them is very intense: they work together, live together on a small compound, worship together and socialise together. It is a tough calling. So why do they do it?

Every member of that team has chosen 'the downward way of Jesus', and living and working in Chad is where the discipleship journey has taken them, at least for now. They could be living comfortable lives with lucrative salaries, surrounded by families and friends in the safety of their own cultures, but they have chosen to follow in the steps of one who, though he was rich, yet for their sakes became poor (2 Corinthians 8:9). Like Jesus, they have 'emptied' themselves and 'humbled' themselves. They are not perfect or without fault: they struggle with the heat, get cross with each other, feel homesick, get frustrated with the culture, lose their focus on God occasionally, and have days when they wonder if it's all worthwhile. They are just normal human beings who have sought to respond as best they can to the call of discipleship as they understand it.

Presumably you are reading this because you too are making a journey of discipleship. Perhaps you are just starting out, with your life ahead of you, and are asking that basic question, 'Lord, what would you have me to do?' If so, don't be afraid of embracing his will wholeheartedly. There is no safer place to be, no happier place, no place more fulfilling and satisfying than in the centre of God's will. Maybe you have been on the road for a long time and feel the need to stop and take your bearings. Remind yourself how you got to where you are now: how did God guide you and how did you know it was his will? Open yourself afresh to his calling, offering yourself again to the doing of his will, whether that be more of the same or something entirely different. All the while, keep your eyes on him, being mindful of the journey he made for you, and seek his grace to continue in the path marked out for you.

If the discipleship journey impinges on our outward lives, the transformational journey, which we now consider, will impact on our inner life. It is not so much about what we do as about who we are and what we are becoming. It is about the growth that is taking place inside of us as we seek to allow the mind and attitude of Christ to be shaped and formed within us, the life of Christ to be expressed through us.

It is so easy for us to place our emphasis on activity, for that is visible, measurable and easy to quantify. It is not quite as easy to measure character change or personality development, and these can be neglected when there is much work to be done and seemingly little time to accomplish everything on our 'to do' list. Spiritual formation takes time and a certain amount of discipline on our part, as we cooperate with the work of the Spirit within us. Sadly, this part of the journey is neglected by many, even though we would be more effective in our work, and happier as people, if we gave sufficient attention to our inner life.

The amazing thing is that Christ wants to replicate his life in us. He wants us to be like him, not by strenuously trying to copy his example but by allowing him to form his own life within us. This was the goal of all Paul's ministry, summed up in his words to the Galatians: 'My dear children, for whom I am again in the pains of childbirth until Christ is formed in you' (Galatians 4:19). There is a process of maturation in the Christian life, which takes us from being children to becoming spiritually mature adults. This process was recognised by the apostle John when he spoke about his readers as children, young men and fathers, indicating the different stages of development (1 John 2:12–14). It was recognised also by Peter, who exhorted his hearers to 'grow in the grace and knowledge of our Lord and Saviour Jesus Christ' (2 Peter 3:18).

The 'downward way of Jesus' is impossible without the inner attitudes of self-emptying and humility that characterised Jesus. The reason Paul shared that hymn with the Philippians was so that this mind of Christ might be formed within them, thereby enabling them to live in harmony and unity of purpose together.

When Jesus washed his disciples' feet in the upper room (John 13:1–17), he not only demonstrated his own servant heart but also gave us an example to follow. He wasn't afraid of doing menial tasks because he was secure in his own identity (v. 3). He had no need to feel superior to others to maintain his dignity, but could humbly adopt the role of a servant without losing his sense of worth or value. To divest himself of the robe (his status, prestige and power) and to take up the towel and basin (the symbols of servanthood, lowliness and meekness) was not difficult for him, for he already had the disposition of a servant. Likewise, because he was filled with love and compassion for them (v. 1), he was able to step outside himself and consider their needs. In other words, he was able to look to the interests of others (Philippians 2:4).

The process of spiritual maturation consists of three important stages. The first stage is that of knowing our identity in Christ, coming to the assurance that we are God's beloved children, loved by him unconditionally and eternally. This gives us our security and self-worth and meets our need for significance. It sets us free from trying vainly to establish a worth of our own, based upon our performance, success or competence. This in turn delivers us from the need to compare ourselves, either favourably or unfavourably, with other people.

The second stage is reached as we become increasingly aware that Christ is now living his life within us. His Spirit has been joined with our spirit, and our bodies have become his temple (1 Corinthians 6:17, 19). Christ, the hope of glory, indwells us: as we yield ourselves to him, he will reproduce his life in us and express that same life through us. For our part, this means learning to live in dependency upon him and ceasing from striving to work for him by our own efforts. It also requires us to remain or 'abide' in him, which we do by the careful practice of the various spiritual disciplines. In this way, and perhaps through the painful process of brokenness, we come to the place where we can say with Paul, 'I no longer live, but Christ lives in me' (Galatians 2:20).

The final stage occurs when we choose the 'downward way' of self-emptying and humility. As the outer shell of self-centredness and self-will is broken within us, so the life of Christ is released through us in an overflow of compassion and love to others. Now the fruit of the Spirit (love, joy, peace and so on: Galatians 5:22–23) is abundantly seen in our lives, his gifts become increasingly operational (1 Corinthians 12:7–12; Romans 12:6–8; 1 Peter 4:8–11) and the impact we make on others becomes greater. Every day requires a renewed decision to live this way, choosing to die to self in order to live for God. This is the journey of transformation that we are on, and we can go as far down the path of Christ-likeness as we choose.

I regularly teach on orientation courses for people going into crosscultural ministry in Africa. It is a joy to see such people stepping out in faith and obedience and responding to the call of God upon their lives, full of enthusiasm for God and expectation of how he will use them. This is the discipleship journey. However, I try to remind them not to forget the other, deeper journey that they are on, that of being transformed into the likeness of Christ, and how the two overlap so often. 'It's not what you will do for God in Africa,' I remind them, 'but what God will do for you in Africa, that really counts.'

Yes, through our service we may have the joy of accomplishing things for him but, more often than not, God's agenda is about making us into the people he wants us to be. Discipleship and transformation go hand in hand.

✥

3

The journey through life

Alongside the metaphor of the journey is that of pilgrimage, a word-picture that is common in both scripture and Christian tradition. A pilgrim is someone on a sacred journey. They do not travel for pleasure, like the tourist, or for gain, like the business person, but because they are seeking God and want to give their whole life to the search to know him more fully.

Some of the heroes of faith listed in Hebrews 11 are described as being pilgrims. They lived their lives by faith, trusting the promises of God and realising that this world was not their real home: 'they admitted that they were aliens and strangers on earth' (v. 13, see also 1 Peter 1:1; 2:11). Likewise, the psalmist speaks about those who have 'set their hearts on pilgrimage' (Psalm 84:5), whose desire for God moves them to journey to Jerusalem to worship him there.

With this perspective, the whole of life becomes part of a sacred journey and everything that happens to us in the course of our lives can be integrated into our walk with God. Thus the psalmist can say, 'These laws of yours have been my source of joy and singing through all these years of my earthly pilgrimage' (Psalm 119:54, LB). The patriarch Jacob shared this viewpoint and, in disclosing his age to Pharaoh, revealed his awareness of the sacredness of life. 'The years of my pilgrimage are a hundred and thirty,' he declared (Genesis 47:9).

The two aspects of journeying that we have considered so far—the discipleship journey and the journey of transformation—take place within the context of everything that is happening to us in life, and in the setting of the particular stage of life through which we are passing. It is important to recognise and take note of the interconnectedness of our faith journey with the season of life we are in, for they have an impact on each other. Knowing where we are on the journey has a lot to do with where we are in life. Each stage of life brings its own special opportunities and also its unique set of challenges. When we see our lives as a sacred journey, it transforms the way we look at what happens to us and how we respond to the circumstances we face.

Five hundred years ago, Shakespeare identified the seven ages of man.[4] More recently, in the 1950s, Erik Erikson developed a model of human development with eight stages, following the progression through life from birth to old age. He suggested that each stage requires us to learn a particular psychological ability before the next stage of maturity can be reached. His focus was mainly on the development of children and teenagers, and society is very different now from the way it was in the 1950s, but Erikson's work still remains the basis for our understanding of the various life stages through which we pass.[5] It is helpful to have such an overview of the phases of life, so that we can more accurately find our bearings. I want to look briefly at normal adult development (rather than childhood, which is vitally important but outside the scope of this book), and how it relates to spiritual growth, basing my thoughts on the work of Peter Feldmeier in *The Developing Christian* and Janet Hagberg and Robert Guelich in *The Critical Journey*.[6]

Early/young adulthood (18–22 years)

This is when the transition is taking place from adolescence into adulthood, which may involve leaving home. It is an exciting stage for some and traumatic for others—a time of intellectual growth (attending university or following other training courses) and experimentation as a way of finding our own personal value system.

Identity is shaped through the discovery of gifting and ability and the assumption of various roles. At this stage it is important to belong to a group and have a network of friends.

Spiritually it may be a barren period for some, but for those with faith it is a time of growth and of being discipled. Full of idealism, many at this stage use their 'gap year' as an opportunity for service, at home or abroad, and this provides a unique opportunity to learn about God's faithfulness, social justice and compassionate caring through vivid personal experience. A community of faith is important, and belonging to the chosen group is taken seriously and with commitment. Faith at this point is propositional, uncritically held and largely untested. It is helpful to have both pace-setters (those who inspire us) and mentors (those who advise us) at this stage.

Adulthood (22–40 years)

This is the period when we become independent people with our own firm values and beliefs. It is a time when a career path is chosen and ambitions followed, and when long-term relationships with the opposite sex may be formed, leading to marriage or (according to one's value system) cohabitation. For many, marriage will lead to parenting and the challenges of moving from individuality and self-gratification to thinking of the needs of others.

Spiritually, this is a time when we need to seek God's will actively because we are making important decisions that will affect the rest of our life. It is a challenging time as we seek to live out our faith with integrity. Couples are learning what it means to have a Christian marriage and how to bring up their children in the faith. Single people are being challenged to maintain sexual purity and to trust God in their relationships. This is also the period when we begin to take on responsibilities and leadership roles in churches and organisations. It is a 'high energy' period, too, in which balancing home and work and church commitments becomes vital.

Middle age (40–65 years)

It has been said that this is the most dramatic period of life, in terms of both human development and spiritual growth. It is a time of appraisal when we ask, 'What have I done with my life?' and it often brings us to a 'fork in the road' where we can either stall or make new progress. Children leave home but ageing parents may become more demanding. All this can create a sense of midlife crisis for some, but for others there is the joyful discovery of their true self, growing financial independence and a new lease of life.

Spiritually this can be a very potent period because it is when the inward journey takes on greater significance and deep transformation can take place. Often the burden of leadership responsibility begins to take its toll, and questions of faith begin to arise—either intellectual ones or those associated with disappointment. Broken dreams and shattered expectations call us deeper. This can lead to a period of spiritual deconstruction, to a 'dark night of the soul', until faith is reformulated and constructed in a new way that makes greater sense. Spiritual direction can be helpful as we navigate the choppy waters of our lives. Those who have made their way through this period may become good mentors of others, and often reach a point of convergence, where who they are and what they do are aligned for maximum effectiveness.

Elderhood (65 years and beyond)

Now that people in developed countries are living longer, this stage has become extended. Retirement marks its beginning and requires the restructuring of life, which can put extra strain on marriages with unresolved problems. One of the challenges over these years is about accepting physical decline and increasing limitations. It can be a period of bereavement and grief as we lose those things that once defined us, and a sense of uselessness can overtake us. At the same time, the realisation of our own mortality increases as friends or spouses die. For those who adapt well, however, this can be a time of caring for others, of listening with wisdom and insight, of being able to accept people and situations with graciousness.

Spiritually, the early years of this period can provide us with new opportunities for ministry and service, and for continued personal growth. As time passes and we experience the changes of age, we have the chance to let God transfigure our sufferings and losses and take us deeper into himself. It can become a period of deep intimacy and communion with God, and we can encourage younger leaders with our wisdom and prayer. Released from the need to achieve and accomplish, we can offer succour and support to those coming behind us. Finally, facing death is an act of faith and can provide an opportunity for reconciliation with others and with ourselves.

Here, then, is an overview of the phases of life through which we may pass. I have only sketched the landscape in outline, but there should be enough here to make you think about your own journey through life and to see its connection with your spiritual growth and development. Where we are at any given moment reflects the intersection between our discipleship journey (doing God's will), our journey of transformation (how we are being changed to become more like Jesus) and our pilgrimage on earth (the life stage through which we are passing).

How does this relate to the idea of working from a place of rest? First, there is a very obvious connection in that we experience a natural diminishing of energy as we move through life. I know that there are glorious exceptions, like Moses (Deuteronomy 34:7), and many older people today have an incredible vitality, but the majority of us recognise the need to slow down as we get older. Whereas in our youth we may serve God out of natural vigour, and therefore inadvertently in our own strength, later we more easily see the wisdom of depending on God's power rather than our own. Once we could not sit still; now we are happy to rest a while. We become more willing to recognise our need for physical rest and to seek the spiritual rest by which we can sustain ministry. Sitting by the well, as Jesus did, is an attractive option!

Second, the journey through life throws up 'seasons of life' and 'windows of opportunity' that we must note as they are integral to our discipleship. There are times when it is better to be in a settled situation (for example, during children's secondary schooling or when we have to care for elderly relatives), and we can rest in the fact that this is part of God's calling, at least for a season in our life, joyfully accepting the limitations placed on us. By contrast, there will also be times when change and transition are possible and even desirable (for example, when we have just graduated or are newly married or when our children have left home), and we can be open to new possibilities of service as we discern God's will for the next phase of life. These are the windows of opportunity, when we can reconsider carefully exactly what kind of work we should be doing.

Finally, it is helpful to recognise that, as we go through life, a process of convergence often takes place. We grow in our understanding of ourselves and of other people; we more accurately identify our gifts and calling; we feel less need to prove ourselves by what we do or achieve; we know what we are good at and what we are not. Thus, our being (who we are) and our doing (what God has made us for) gradually come together in greater harmony than ever before, so that from midlife onwards we can enter the most fruitful years of our lives. We learn to work from a place of rest in the sense that we choose to do that for which God made us. When such a convergence is reached, it is a place of deep satisfaction, when we are at our most effective and efficient.

Reflection

- Think of your life in terms of the journey metaphor.
  - Where are you on your journey through life?
  - Where are you on your discipleship journey?
  - Where are you on your journey of transformation?

Notice how the three journeys flow into each other and overlap.

- As you look back over the way you have come, what have you learnt:
  - about yourself?
  - about God?
  - about the nature of Christian ministry?

- As you look to the way before you, how do you feel?
  - What challenges lie ahead?
  - What opportunities can you see?
  - Do you anticipate any changes?

- Find some photos of yourself that depict the stages of your life from childhood through to the present. Lay them out in order and prayerfully meditate on them. What does God show you?

It's natural to feel tired
on the journey

4

The humanity of Jesus

When we meet Jesus at the well, we encounter him in his humanity. After the early start and the long morning walking through the countryside, he is tired and needing a rest. He does what any of us would do: he looks for a comfortable place to sit for a while and take the weight off his feet. Not only that, but he is thirsty and in need of a drink. He is probably hot and sweaty as the midday sun beats down on him, and his throat is dry and parched. He longs for something cool and refreshing. Have you ever known thirst like that? There is also an implication that, like the disciples who are with him, he has worked up an appetite on the walk and is feeling a little bit peckish, which is why they have gone into the town to buy food. Tired, thirsty and hungry—the hallmarks of someone who is truly human, just like us.

I find the humanity of Jesus as portrayed in the Gospels immensely reassuring. Christian doctrine tells us that Jesus was fully God and yet fully man. He is able to bring God and humanity together, since he is the perfect bridge between us. The fact that he entered our world and lived our life gives us confidence to believe that he really does understand us and can represent us effectively before his Father. He has identified himself with us, and therefore we can identify with him. We can approach him because he is one of us.

The writer to the Hebrews makes it clear that only someone who shares our humanity could save us. In the work of 'bringing many sons to glory' he must suffer as we suffer; he must be part of the human family and become our brother. If he is to rescue us from the devil's grip, he must share our flesh and blood: he has to be made like us in every way. Only then can he take up the role of being our merciful and faithful high priest. Having suffered and been tempted himself, he is able to help us when we are tempted (see Hebrews 2:10–18).

If we are to draw near to God with confidence, it will be because we understand that Jesus was fully man as well as fully God. We need to know that he will deal with us gently when we face our own temptations, and even when we sin he will respond to us in grace and mercy. Someone who had no understanding of what it is to be human might be harsh and unreasonable with us, scolding us for our weakness and berating us for our inconsistencies. Then we would have no encouragement to draw near. As it is, because he has been tempted but without sinning, he is able to help and strengthen us in our times of need (see Hebrews 4:14–16).

It will be worthwhile, therefore, taking time to dwell on the humanity of Jesus and make a strong connection with the one who has so completely identified himself with us. A proper realisation of his humanity will release us to acknowledge our own humanity, with its weaknesses and limitations, and to receive from him the strength we need to live our lives in this fallen world.

Jesus was born of his mother Mary in a way that was supernatural and yet quite normal. In that miracle of Holy Spirit activity, his tiny form was shaped within her womb in just the same way as we were in our mothers' wombs. He entered the world into the dim light of the stable at Bethlehem, as helpless as any other newborn infant, with the same need to be nurtured and nourished at his mother's breast. Despite the carol's insistence that 'the little Lord Jesus, no crying he makes', his healthy lungs would have helped him announce his arrival and signal when he was hungry or needed changing.

Slowly, as the weeks and months passed, he began to grow, subject to all the normal laws of human development—learning to walk, learning to talk, learning to feed himself, falling and scraping his knees, knocking things over, needing to be watched all the time.

He would have been inquisitive and adventurous, full of bound-less energy, a typical toddler. Luke the physician, in particular, seems interested in all of this. 'And the child grew,' he reports, 'and became strong; he was filled with wisdom, and the grace of God was upon him' (Luke 2:40).

The years pass by and, in the village of Nazareth, Jesus is twelve years old and on the edge of adolescence. Almost his entire childhood is hidden from us, but the story of his visit to the temple in Jerusalem for the Passover (Luke 2:41–52) opens a window for us into the world of 'the boy Jesus' (v. 43). How excited he must have been to visit the capital city, travelling 'in caravan' with other relatives and friends on the long journey south. Yet it is not the sights and sounds of the city that capture the young boy's attention. Rather, he is to be found sitting with the temple teachers, listening to them and asking questions of a spiritual nature. The consciousness of who he really is and the destiny ahead of him seems to be breaking in upon him, even at this early age. It was obviously a growing understanding, in keeping with his natural development, but there is no mistaking his increasing awareness of his special relationship with God. 'Didn't you know I had to be in my Father's house?' he asks, by way of explanation to his parents (v. 49), who are worried by his absence from the returning group.

Once again, Luke (who seems to have depended upon Mary herself for these insights) recognises the natural development taking place within the boy. 'But his mother treasured all these things in her heart. And Jesus grew in wisdom and stature, and in favour with God and men' (vv. 51–52). Nothing can be rushed, and there can be no short cuts to the changes that must take place within him as he matures from boy to man. There will be another 18 years of silent obscurity before he is ready for his ministry.

When eventually his public ministry begins, it does so with two significant events, both of which underline his humanity. First, he is baptised by John in the Jordan, not because of any need to repent of his sins but because of his willingness to identify himself with those he has come to save (see Luke 3:21–22). Second, he is led by the Spirit into the wilderness to be tempted by the devil. This is a real encounter with the one who is the personification of evil, and the battle is fierce. Simply because he is human, Jesus can feel the pull of temptation. Each of the three devilish suggestions is targeted at potential human weak spots—physical need, the appetite for power and the love of the spectacular. Each time Jesus resists, strengthened by the Spirit and guided by his knowledge of the scripture. He has been tempted 'in every way' as we are (Hebrews 4:15) and has come through victorious. There will be other skirmishes with the enemy, but for now Jesus has proved his ability to resist temptation.

So the period of public activity gets underway, and for three years he will crisscross the country proclaiming the kingdom. Through the lens of the Gospel writers, we are given an intimate portrait of what he was like, based either on first-hand experience or the reports of others close to him. John confirms that they encountered a real man, albeit one who was also God: 'that which was from the beginning, which we have heard, which we have seen with our eyes, which we have looked at and our hands have touched,' he says (1 John 1:1). For him, the mark of authentic Christianity is the affirmation that Jesus really was human: 'This is how you can recognise the Spirit of God: every spirit that acknowledges that Jesus Christ has come in the flesh is from God' (4:2).

The person of Jesus revealed to us in the Gospel narratives is one who is wonderfully human. Physically he is strong, able to walk long distances, spend 40 days fasting in the desert and keep up a hectic schedule. He still gets tired, as we have seen, and needs to sleep to restore his energy levels (Mark 4:38). His physical body requires care and attention like any other, even though it is a body prepared by God for him (Hebrews 10:5) and one in which the fullness of God resides (Colossians 2:9).

Like any normal person, Jesus had a strong emotional life. He appears first and foremost as a joyful and fun-loving person, one 'anointed with the oil of joy' beyond his companions (Hebrews 1:9; Luke 10:21; John 15:11). Yet he is able to enter deeply into the feelings of others, being moved with great compassion for those in need (Matthew 9:36; 14:14; 15:32; 20:34). Sometimes he is indignant at injustice and wrongdoing. (Mark 3:5; 10:14). Often he is moved to tears by his love for others (John 11:33; Luke 19:41). Here is the 'man of sorrows, and familiar with suffering' of whom the prophet Isaiah had spoken (Isaiah 53:3).

As a man, Jesus enjoyed and needed the companionship of others. He needed to receive the affirmation and love that come through human friendship. Yes, he knew unreservedly that he was the object of the Father's love (Matthew 3:17) and this was the foundation of his identity, but, like us, he also enjoyed the intimacy of close friendship. I think he enjoyed 'being with the lads' (as we might call his disciples), especially the trio of Peter, James and John, who seem to have been his closest friends. Of course, John was one who 'leaned on his bosom' (John 13:23; 21:20, KJV) during the last supper in an expression of friendship and closeness. Think, too, of the welcome he received, and delighted in, at the Bethany home of Mary, Martha and Lazarus.

I am especially struck by his encounter with the woman at the house of Simon the Pharisee (Luke 7:36–50). He seems not at all embarrassed by her public display of affection; he appears even to have revelled in it and welcomed the loving touch, the soothing washing of his feet, the gentle application of the refreshing perfume. Indeed, he says as much to his host: 'Do you see this woman? I came into your house. You did not give me any water for my feet, but she wet my feet with her tears and wiped them with her hair. You did not give me a kiss, but this woman, from the time I entered, has not stopped kissing my feet. You did not put oil on my head, but she has poured perfume on my feet' (vv. 44–46).

During his life on earth, Jesus related to God as a human being, in the same way that we do. That is why—surprisingly, perhaps— we find him at prayer so often. He was completely dependent upon

God and needed to receive divine strength for the task ahead of him (Luke 6:12; 9:28). He was led by the Spirit, empowered by the Spirit and anointed by the Spirit (4:1, 14, 18), showing by his example what it means for a man or woman to live in fellowship with God, and what can be accomplished when we yield to the Spirit.

Every step of his journey from the manger to the cross was made by the deliberate choice of obedience. Never once did he falter from doing the Father's will, no matter what it cost him. At no time was the reality of his human choice more keenly felt than in the garden of Gethsemane, where he agonised over his future. 'During the days of Jesus' life on earth, he offered up prayers and petitions with loud cries and tears to the one who could save him from death,' says the writer to the Hebrews, 'and he was heard because of his reverent submission. Although he was a son, he learned obedience from what he suffered' (Hebrews 5:7–8). His continually chosen obedience came out of a will fully surrendered to God, not from some automated programme inside him, and was the basis of his righteous life. Jesus succeeded where Adam failed (see Romans 5:18–19).

Because he was human, Jesus could feel pain, and this is what makes his death on the cross all the more amazing and inspiring. Remember that the word 'excruciating' comes from the same root as the word 'crucify', and it tells us something of the agony he experienced as he 'tasted' death—felt it in every fibre of his being—for each one of us (Hebrews 2:9). Mel Gibson's graphic portrayal of the crucifixion in his film *The Passion of the Christ* brings this home to us with chilling reality. What courage he displayed, what sacrifice he made! Through the offering of his physical body on the cross, he reconciled us to God and opened for us a new and living way into the holy presence (Colossians 1:22; Hebrews 10:19–22).

All of this is what qualifies him now to serve as our great high priest. God raised him from the dead and exalted him, crowning him with glory and honour. He is at the right hand of God, interceding for us and hearing our cries for help. Because he has lived our life and walked where we walk, he can understand our need and match it with his grace.

Bishop J.C. Ryle summed it up well when he said this: 'He knows the heart of a weary man',[7] and we would quickly add, 'and a weary woman also'. If he was tired on his own journey, he is not taken aback when we find ourselves weary and exhausted with life. He knows what it is like. He has been there; he has felt it. We need not be ashamed of our tiredness or feel that we have failed because we are worn out. We do not have to cover it up, put on a brave face or pretend it isn't happening. We can come just as we are—in the words of the hymn, weary, worn and sad—and find in him a resting place.

✧

— 5 —

Ready to drop?

One of the most often quoted passages from Eugene Peterson's paraphrase of the Bible, THE MESSAGE, contains these wonderful words from Matthew 11:28–30:

'Are you tired? Worn out? Burned out on religion? Come to me. Get away with me and you'll recover your life. I'll show you how to take a real rest. Walk with me and work with me—watch how I do it. Learn the unforced rhythms of grace. I won't lay anything heavy or ill-fitting on you. Keep company with me and you'll learn to live freely and lightly.'

Not only has Peterson captured the essence of what Jesus is saying here and put his thoughts into contemporary language, but he has also captured the mood and heart-cry of many of God's people in these frantic days in which we live.

When we read these words, we may want to respond out loud. 'Are you tired?' 'Yes, often,' we want to reply. In fact, most of us live with tiredness as our constant companion and never feel able to shrug off its weighty presence. Our lives are so full, and we are so stretched, that we are never anything but tired. 'Are you worn out?' 'Pretty much,' we answer. We have given and given, and there is often little left in reserve. When we do manage to rest, there never seems to be enough time to restore ourselves fully, so we can slide even further down the slippery slope of exhaustion. The demands don't lessen and the responsibilities don't go away, so we press on, pushing ourselves to do more. 'Are you burned out on religion?' 'Not yet,' we respond, but inside we are worried. We don't like to admit it but we are almost there. We know we are sailing close to the wind, continually operating at maximum capacity with little respite, often living on the brink of collapse. The religious system in which we operate doesn't always help, either, demanding more and more commitment from us while paying little attention to our need for rest. We find ourselves joyless, resentful and lacking motivation.

Is this what God intended for us? I don't think so! The words of Jesus remind us that there is another way to live, a better way to do ministry. He invites us into a totally different way of being, to what I have called 'working from a place of rest'. He asks us to look at how he does things and to follow his example. He welcomes us into a collaboration with himself—sharing in the work, with him as the senior partner. He promises to teach us how to operate in this new way of living so that we can discover for ourselves the incredible freedom and lightness that result from being joined with him and living according to the rhythm of his grace.

Tired; exhausted; burnt out—these are the words that, sadly, many of us would use to describe our state of being much of the time. Why is this? In part, it is due to the demands of the world in which we live. Western culture in particular has enjoyed the benefits of modernity—better health care, more food, advances in science and technology, greater access to information, increasing affluence, cheaper travel—and yet we remain dissatisfied, depressed and weary. The promise of labour-saving devices and technology to reduce our workload seems to have backfired. Instead, our working lives have accelerated and expanded. More is demanded of us and in less time. Productivity is the key word and performance the indicator. We find ourselves working longer hours and squeezing more in. Mobile phones and internet access mean we are available all the time, wherever we are, and our 24/7 society leaves little time for rest. We are experiencing what has been described as an 'exhaustion epidemic', in which, according to journalist Louise Carpenter, 'exhaustion is now integral to our lifestyles'.[8]

The culture of the world in which we live does not, by itself, account for our hyperactive lifestyles. There are also pressures within each of us that drive us to perform and achieve. Often it is because we measure our worth by what we produce: we need to be successful to prove to ourselves that we are significant, that our lives matter. Sometimes we are driven by acquisitiveness and greed, wanting a better lifestyle and being willing to pay the price of overcommitment to reach our goals. Often we push ourselves too hard because we are ashamed to say that we cannot cope, and afraid of failing in the eyes of others, of being regarded as 'weak'. Some of us need to be needed and feed off the demands that others make of us, to the detriment of our own well-being. It is a complex cocktail of internal and external factors that pressurises us into drivenness.

Those who work in Christian ministry are not immune. In fact, many of the above factors motivate us as well, but in addition we may hold what is called the 'Protestant work ethic' (the belief that it is godly to be hardworking) as well as a heightened sense of loyalty, conscientiousness and responsibility. Our personal theology, too, may assure us that it is noble to 'spend and be spent' for the cause of Christ, and that we should give ourselves unstintingly to the cause. Some Christian organisations unconsciously exploit these noble characteristics in their staff, creating by their overambitious plans an impossible workload. The needs all around us are so great, and the work is never done.

Many churches operate in a very similar way. For some reason, we tend to try to do more than we can resource, nobly pressing on in the name of 'faith', asking more and more of the devoted few. Small churches are as guilty as large ones but it is often the mega-churches where staff are under most pressure. Church growth thinking has influenced us to the extent that the only criterion we use to measure effectiveness is numerical growth, so the pressure to produce results (and keep producing them) is enormous. Everything must be done to 'excellence' as well, so unacknowledged perfectionism becomes another demanding factor. In one church, a group of exhausted staff members tried to reason with their leader, asking him to slow down the pace, but found no compassion. 'We're all under pressure,' he replied. 'You'll just have to learn how to cope.'

Where, then, can we draw the line? When can we say that we have finished for the day? When we stop and notice Jesus sitting by the well, we are liberated by the reality of his humanity and experience of fatigue to affirm our own humanity, and to recognise that we, too, have limits. We are not machines; we are human beings. We cannot keep producing the goods without respite. We need a break. We need to sit by the well.

Our compassionate God is well aware of our humanity because he created and made us. 'He knows how we are formed, he remembers that we are dust,' says the psalmist (Psalm 103:14). Like the tender Father he is, he knows the limitations of his children, and he does not ask of us more than we can give, even if others do. Rather, his promise is this: 'I will refresh the weary and satisfy the faint' (Jeremiah 31:25).

Nowhere is this brought out more clearly than in Isaiah 40. Here we are presented with a picture of the greatness of the Creator God, who himself does not grow tired or weary (v. 28). By contrast, we are also presented with a picture of our own humanity, with its frail limitations. We do grow tired and weary, and even young men in the prime of their lives suffer from exhaustion (v. 30). But the prophet also paints for us a picture where the two come together in an amazing divine exchange, where the strength of the Creator is poured into the weakness of the created, enabling them to soar like eagles, carried along by a strength that is not their own (vv. 29, 31). How does this happen? It happens when they take time to hope in the Lord (v. 31), or, as it is also translated, to 'wait upon the Lord' (KJV).

Is it reading too much into the Gospel story to suggest that, when Jesus was sitting by the well, he was in fact waiting upon God and allowing his own strength to be renewed? Far from suggesting that we should keep going because the Lord will give us strength, Isaiah is telling us that it is essential to take time out to practise this waiting upon God. Without quiet moments of reaching out to God in the midst of our busy days, tiredness will overwhelm us.

Affirming our own humanity means recognising that we live with limitations. Our energy level is like a bank account. First we must put something in and then we can draw something out. We cannot draw out more than has been deposited. If we continue to be active without stopping to be re-energised, eventually our account will be overdrawn. This is what we mean by exhaustion and burn-out.

Someone has put it like this: if your output exceeds your input, eventually the shortfall will be your downfall. 'Output' is our involvement in the activities of life and ministry. It does not matter who we are or how much we enjoy what we do, external activity requires the spending of energy, and that is output. Likewise, time spent with God or in rest (sleep) or recreation are ways of putting back what the day has taken out, restoring energy. This is 'input'. If we give out more than we take in, then we arrive at a place of 'shortfall', where the demands on us are greater than our resources to cope. This is where fatigue begins to set in. If this state of imbalance continues, we will arrive at a state of exhaustion and then burn-out, which is 'downfall'. It could mean the end of our ministry, or at least a temporary curtailment.

In reflecting on this helpful little equation, I came up with my own more positive version: if your input exceeds your output, then the excess will be your wellness. If we can manage our energy level in such a way that we have some spare capacity, then we will live in a state of well-being. We will be more relaxed, have greater creativity, live in better health, generally be more effective and actually become more productive. The challenge is to have the confidence to recognise our own limitations and not to take on too much. This may seem unnatural and selfish at first, especially to those who are used to giving out all the time, but it is the only way to ensure we finish the course. I often say to those involved in ministry, 'Remember, we are in this for the long haul, not just a short season.' Managing our energy level is a crucial factor in sustaining ministry down the years in the challenging circumstances that many of us face.

The Bible says that Elijah was 'a man just like us' (James 5:17). In other words, he was human with limitations. After the triumph on Mount Carmel, we find him lonely and afraid, running away to hide in a cave, exhausted and depressed (1 Kings 19:3–9). It was a normal human response to excessive and demanding activity, and we can identify with his weakness. Nor is the prophet alone among the biblical giants in his humanity. Gideon, pursuing his enemies, finds himself and his men exhausted (Judges 8:4). David, worn down by Shimei's barrage of abuse, arrives at his destination exhausted (2 Samuel 16:13–14). Daniel, too, overwhelmed by the pressures he is under, succumbs to exhaustion and falls ill in bed (Daniel 8:27).

To be human is to experience tiredness. It is natural and we should not be ashamed or embarrassed to admit our need. The humanity of Jesus reminds us that he understands and cares, and is there for us in our time of need.

❖

Margin

I like to think that I am not a driven person, but the reality is that I am an achiever. I seek to find my identity in Christ and to derive my sense of worth and value from the fact of my belovedness, the knowledge that I am loved unconditionally and unchangeably by God. I know that I am not defined by what I do, yet I still find myself overcommitted. There are times when I look at my diary and sigh deeply inside. 'Why do I do this?' I ask myself.

Part of my own problem is that I enjoy my work as a freelance trainer immensely. I am energised by being out there, meeting new people, and I'm excited by new opportunities. Since I am a self-employed person, I am aware that I need to work in order to live, so turning down invitations is far from easy. Having time off means I am neither achieving nor earning! The result is that my diary is usually overfull and I have difficulty controlling it. I have two temptations in particular. One is to not leave enough 'recovery time' after events and overseas trips. The other is to squeeze commitments into an already crowded schedule in order to catch key opportunities or avoid letting someone down.

I shared my situation with a peer mentoring group that I belong to, all experienced people involved in 'member care' (that is, looking after those in Christian ministry overseas). They gave me some helpful feedback. 'Make sure you know your priorities,' said one. 'Do only that which you can do,' offered another. 'Think about what within you might be feeding this,' challenged someone else. Yet another suggested I look at how I could multiply what I am doing by working with another person. A final contributor advised me not to accept invitations on the spur of the moment, but to wait and process things first. This was all very helpful and it was really encouraging to be heard and have my concern validated by the group, as well as to be prayed for afterwards. Looking back on my notes, though, I saw that someone had mentioned the word 'margin', and, although it didn't strike me so forcibly at the time, subsequently it was this thought that helped me the most.

Not long after this peer group meeting, God spoke to me through an Old Testament story and an ancient Jewish custom. I was reminded of the book of Ruth and the story of how Boaz commanded his harvesters not to reap to the very edge of the fields, but to leave some of the gleanings for the poor (Ruth 2:1–9; see also Leviticus 19:9). I felt God saying to me that I was trying to reap to the very edge of my 'field' and that I should not be afraid to leave some 'margin' at the edges, for the benefit of both myself and others. He seemed to say that I must not feel I had to fill every slot in my diary, but that I should learn to leave some white space, to have more time for rest, recovery and creativity. I also felt his reassurance that I would not miss out either professionally or financially by doing this.

According to Dr Richard Swenson, margin is 'the space between our load and our limits'.[9] It is the opposite of being overloaded. Swenson describes how, due to the demands made upon us by so-called progress, many of us live with the pain of overload. We are overloaded in many areas of our lives by attempting too much, facing too much change, having to make too many choices and being too committed. We are overwhelmed by too much noise, too much information, too much traffic and too many people. We bear the brunt of too many expectations, have too much work to be done and carry too much debt. We have too little time and not enough energy. 'We do not have an inexhaustible source of human energy,' he says. 'Limits are real, and despite what some might think, limits are not even an enemy. Overloading is the enemy.'[10]

The great danger in this is that we do not always realise when we are overloaded. Each of us has our own capacity for load-bearing and, along with it, our particular threshold—the extent we can reach without becoming overloaded. However, it is not always easy to recognise when we are going beyond our threshold, because the signals can be hard to discern. We seem to be coping very well but then something happens—often a small and trivial incident in itself—that triggers a disproportionate reaction in us. We suddenly find ourselves becoming angry, defensive, emotional and upset. While some people have an outburst, others turn inwards and withdraw in sullen despair. Sometimes we can recover our composure but sometimes we can't, and that is when we realise how seriously overloaded we are. Burn-out does not send a calling card in advance. It creeps up unawares and takes even the most resilient by surprise.

The price we pay for overloaded living should be obvious—inner tension and unhappiness, strain on relationships, poor health, decreasing motivation, breakdown, spiritual lethargy and so on—yet we continue to push ourselves too hard. We are like Gideon's army, 'exhausted yet keeping up the pursuit' (Judges 8:4). We fail to establish boundaries for ourselves and allow the demands of our work and the needs of other people to swamp us. We add new responsibilities on top of old ones without ever removing anything, so our pile gets higher and higher. The inability to say 'No' to others robs us of the freedom to say 'Yes' to what God wants us to do.

Very few people can thrive on marginless living. Having margin means having something in reserve for contingencies and unanticipated situations. It means we have time and energy to use at our own discretion. Swenson suggests that we need to develop margin in at least four key areas of our lives—emotional energy, physical energy, time and finances. For the sake of our health and well-being we should not overextend ourselves in any of these areas. Of the four, he considers margin in emotional energy to be the most important.

It is apparent from the fact that Jesus had no hesitation in sitting down to rest and 'waste' a few minutes, doing nothing in particular, that he knew how to live with 'margin' in the area of his time. Later, when the Samaritan villagers respond to him, he is able to stay two more days, even at short notice. It seems that he did not live to a tight, overcrowded schedule but had the flexibility to respond to the situation. We recognise his emotional margin, for he appears relaxed and at peace and has the capacity for conversation with a very needy stranger. He is able to see beyond himself and his own concerns, to listen to the cares of another. The picture that emerges of him throughout the Gospels is of someone who lived with a relaxed purposefulness and a clear sense of his priorities, but always having space for those around him. Yes, he is tired at this moment, but he is aware of his tiredness and does not hesitate to take a breather. He is conscious of the need to maintain physical margin through appropriate rest. Financial margin is not something that immediately affects this particular scenario, but again, looking at the Gospel stories as a whole, we know that he was content to live a simple life and trust the Father for his provision. He was not anxious about material concerns.

What about ourselves? Do we have emotional margin? It is so easy for those who are carers of others to neglect their own welfare. We give ourselves to other people—listening to their hurts, mending their wounds—yet fail to care for ourselves. Do we have physical margin? Do we take sufficient time for rest and sleep, for recreation and leisure, for exercise and fun, or do we feel that we must always be on the go, doing something useful and productive? Can we appreciate that it is legitimate to take care of ourselves and our bodies? Do we have time margin? Are we always in a hurry, trying to do everything as quickly as possible? Are we ruled by the clock, slaves to our schedules? Or do we have the time to be spontaneous, to slow down and relax, to be interrupted by God. Finally, do we have financial margin? Do we find ourselves locked into consumerism, overspending and surviving on credit? Have we learnt to live within our means, to practise contentment, to live simply and be wise stewards of what we have? Can we give as well as get, and be generous with what we have?

In Jesus, the Word became flesh and dwelt among us (John 1:14). As a man, Jesus was aware of his natural limitations and lived within them. We too have limits because we too are human, and we are wise to recognise our own limits and adjust accordingly. As Swenson has said, 'It is God the Creator who has made limits, and it is the same God who placed them within us for our protection. We exceed them at our peril.'[11]

Reflection

- Consider the formula given in Chapter 5 (p. 47) and apply it to yourself.
  - What is your current output?
  - What is your current input?
  - Is there a shortfall?
  - If so, are there any signs of a possible downfall?

- What margin is there in your life? How can you create some?
  - Emotional?
  - Physical?
  - Time?
  - Financial?

It's permissible to stop and
rest on the journey

— 7 —

The discipline of stopping

We are slowly building up a picture of what it means to work from a place of rest, by reflecting on the example of Jesus at the well in the Samaritan village of Sychar. We have noted that he was on a journey, returning from Judea northwards to Galilee. Spiritually he was on a much bigger journey, one that had brought him from heaven to earth and would take him back to heaven again via the cross. We have seen, too, that as a result of the journey and his own humanity, he was now feeling tired and in need of rest.

I have to confess that my immediate reaction when I visualised this moment was to say, 'Come on, Jesus, get a move on. There's so much to do and so little time to do it. You have to save the world, and you've only got three years!' This reveals my own impatience and fear of 'wasting' time. Jesus, however, was not in a hurry and never operated out of the fear that he might not finish everything. He knew the importance of stopping, of pausing along the way to be refreshed. By his example, he gives us permission to do the same.

When we sit down, we take the weight off our feet and we are able to rest. When we stop what we are doing, we are able to recharge our batteries and be refreshed. Jesus exemplifies for us the importance of physical rest in order to meet the demands of our calling. He was aware of his own tiredness and he knew the remedy. More than that, he had the freedom to stop what he was doing because he was in a place of spiritual rest. He was able to entrust the successful outcome of his earthly mission into his Father's hands, and did not fear stepping back from its demands for a while. In no sense was he driven by the fear of failure, the size of the task,

56

the enormity of the responsibility or the time constraints upon him. He was free to rest because he trusted in the Father's presence, help and enabling. Thus he was able to work from (or out of) a place of rest, living with the relaxed posture of faith.

The opposite of working from a place of rest is to work from a place of anxiety, and, if we are honest, this is where much of our own feverish activity originates. We have the feeling that we are on our own, that everything depends upon us, and so we had better try our best and work our hardest. Psalm 127 describes this lifestyle perfectly: 'It is in vain that you rise up early and go late to rest, eating the bread of anxious toil,' says the wise king Solomon (v. 2, NRSV). We have all done it, haven't we? Because the day's demands are heavy, we think we will make an early start in order to get on top of things, so we set the alarm earlier than normal and extend our day at the beginning. Then, because deadlines are pressing, we decide to work late and extend the end of our day as well, toiling long into the night in order to finish. Thus we burn the candle at both ends and wind up exhausted because we have missed out on our sleep, the essential ingredient in a rested and balanced life. When we feel there are not enough hours in the day, it's easy to try to borrow a few, isn't it? As a one-off strategy in a busy period it is workable, but as a lifestyle (and that is what it quickly becomes) it is a disaster.

Solomon reminds us that God 'grants sleep to those he loves' (v. 2). Sleep is a gift from God, the natural way by which we restore lost energy. Most people need between seven and eight hours per night as a rule, and the rhythm of work and sleep matches that of day and night in the natural order of things. This is how God designed us to work and we tamper with his rhythm at our peril. I find personally that managing my sleep pattern is vital in coping with the demands upon my life. Having good sleep is one of the most effective ways of ensuring that my input exceeds my output and that I can work hard without being overwhelmed.

Solomon also reminds us that the work does not depend upon us. It is God's work and therefore his responsibility. Unaided human effort will never accomplish the purpose of God. We ought to remember that this is collaboration, with God as the senior partner. 'Unless the Lord builds the house, its builders labour in vain. Unless the Lord watches over the city, the watchmen stand guard in vain' (v. 1). We desperately need to grasp this sobering truth about the limitations of our independent endeavours. Unless God is behind what we are doing, we may as well not bother, for our best efforts will never produce the results for which God is looking. Ambitious achievers (builders) and responsible carers (watchmen), please take note! We were created to depend upon God, and we are most effective when we allow him to work in us and through us.

To sit and relax, we must be able to trust God with our workload. It requires faith to stop in the midst of a heavy schedule but we must be willing to do so, if we are to wait upon God and draw our strength from him. In order to work from a place of rest, we must, like Jesus, practise the discipline of stopping. We must shed the feeling that we have to be always on the go, making the most of the time, doing as much as possible. We need to give ourselves permission to slow down and breathe more deeply. It is not easy, for these habits of hyperactivity are deeply ingrained in our thinking.

A Singaporean friend of mine confessed to finding it almost impossible to rest. She explained her thought process like this.

When I was younger I was brought up by my grandmother. Whenever she saw me doing nothing, like reading a book or gazing out of the window, she would say to me, 'Ai Ling, find something useful to do.' So I would, and now whenever I go to sit down and relax I hear her voice saying, 'Find something useful to do', and I feel compelled to get up and do something, anything.

Can you identify with Ai Ling's compulsion to busyness? Many of us can, which is why we need to see Jesus sitting by the well and receive from his example the permission to sit and do nothing.

The discipline of stopping requires more than a degree of faith.

It requires us to change the way we think about time, to renew our minds. Most of us in the Western world have formulated our attitude towards time in the context of the industrial modern world. We have grown up with the view that 'time is money' (Benjamin Franklin). This is the dictum that shapes the way business and commerce operate. It means that we must never waste time but must strive for efficiency and make the very best use of it. Time is a resource, a commodity to be managed to make us more productive and thereby more profitable. This thinking has given rise to the 24/7 culture in which shops and businesses want to trade without boundaries to maximise their efficiency and increase their incomes.

Most of us are steeped in this way of thinking, and the church, by and large, has also bought into the time-management philosophy of 'get more done in even less time'. All this makes us want to do things more quickly, to speed life up and to cram as many tasks as we can into our day. We want to 'redeem the time', to make good use of the hours we have, to be as busy as everyone else.

I was mulling over the expression 'redeeming the time' recently, and decided to check it out. It is taken from Ephesians 5:16, and is translated in the NIV as 'making the most of every opportunity'—a translation that reflects the cultural conditioning we have just been thinking about. I discovered that the Greek word used in this verse (*exagoradzo*) means literally 'to rescue from loss or misapplication, to buy out of the hands of someone'. Even more literally, it means 'to buy back from the marketplace' (*agora* means 'marketplace'). So what Paul is saying here is not 'Try to get more done in even less time', but exactly the opposite. He is saying, 'Don't let your idea of time be conditioned by the marketplace, but rescue it and use it in God's way.'

God's attitude towards time is very different from that of business, industry and commerce. In his economy, we always have enough time to do what he asks of us. If we feel we are short of time, it is likely that we have taken on work that he has not asked us to do. In his way of operating, we have time to restore our souls, to be still and know that he is God (Psalm 46:10). If we are too busy to rest, it is because we are driving ourselves too hard. In his kingdom, we can walk with a relaxed calmness because he is in control. If we are rushed and harassed, it is because we ourselves are trying to make things happen. This doesn't mean that we shouldn't manage our time well or seek to work efficiently. It simply means that we use our time and establish our priorities from a different value system. We give our time back to God, for him to apportion as he desires.

The discipline of stopping is based upon the twin foundations of our ability to trust God for our work and a renewed attitude towards time. Here is my simple definition of what it means: 'Stopping is pausing for a few minutes, or a few hours, or a few days, to remember who I am, why I am here, and to receive strength for the next part of the journey.'[12] We stop for the purpose of becoming more aware of our true identity as God's beloved children, to clarify our purpose in life and to reconnect with God in such a way as to receive the flow of his divine strength into our lives. Far from doing nothing, stopping is a positive activity, and I think this is exactly what Jesus was doing as he sat by the well. He was resting physically but also connecting with the Father in a way that re-energised him for all that lay ahead.

As my definition suggests, we can stop for a brief moment in order to recentre ourselves upon God. Even in the busiest of days, we may be able to begin with a few minutes of prayerful contemplation before we launch out into the hurly-burly. We can find pools of stillness along the way, too, perhaps as we drive to an appointment, wait in a queue or pause over a coffee break or lunch hour. Then, at the end of the day, even as our head hits the pillow, we can review the day, gratefully identify God's working in our lives and commit ourselves afresh to him.

When possible, longer times of stopping can be part of our rhythm. With discipline and understanding, we can intentionally set aside a few hours in the week to nurture our relationship with

God. A morning or evening spent in quiet reflection can actually multiply our effectiveness, for not only will it refresh us but it will enable us to clarify our priorities and develop our strategies. This is where the principle of sabbath fits in, and we shall devote the next chapter to considering its importance and benefits.

Finally, we can set aside a few days for retreat every now and then—if possible, on an annual basis. In the context of our lives as a whole, it will prove to be a wise investment of time. Slowing down like this will help us avoid the danger of forming our identity through what we do, and will relieve us of the burden of thinking that everything depends upon us. To press the pause button on our activities deliberately, in order to hear from God about our purpose and direction, will supply rich dividends.

When my wife and I were applying to join a mission agency, we were required to spend three weeks being 'assessed' at the national headquarters. The mission home was run by a rather formidable retired missionary, who had a very soft centre underneath her intimidating exterior. She was also a deeply spiritual woman and I have never forgotten one piece of advice she gave to us as new recruits. 'The missionaries who stay the longest on the field,' she said, 'are those who have their afternoon cup of tea!' Now that is a peculiarly British approach to life, and you may have to contextualise it (a can of Coke, maybe?), but it is a piece of homespun wisdom that has worked for me. It does so because it gives us permission to stop and sit, even for a few minutes.

We must make room in our schedules for our own times of sitting by the well. We can do so free from guilt and the pressure to produce or perform. Liberated by the example of Jesus, we can take time to be refreshed and restored, finding the balance that our overcrowded lives need so that we can sustain ministry over the long haul. Finding our own still points, we can establish a place of intimacy with God, out of which can flow a life of fruitful activity.

8

Remember the Sabbath?

This may seem a strange question to ask, but it is an extremely pertinent one. Whatever happened to the Sabbath? A practice that was once integral to Christian living is now largely neglected in Western Christianity, submerged beneath the waves of relentless activity and buried under the weight of the secular mindset, which sees each day as the same. In letting go of the Sabbath, we have lost something very precious. It is time to restore to our lives one of God's greatest gifts of grace.

To understand the Sabbath, we need to go back to the creation story. Having finished his creative work on the sixth day, God chose to rest on the seventh. 'By the seventh day God had finished the work he had been doing; so on the seventh day he rested from all his work. And God blessed the seventh day and made it holy, because on it he rested from all the work of creating that he had done' (Genesis 2:2–3). Why did God need to rest? Because he was tired? No. As we have seen in Isaiah 40, the living God never grows tired or weary (v. 28). He neither slumbers nor sleeps (Psalm 121:3–4). God chose to rest, not because he needed to but in order to establish a pattern for us to follow, showing us the balance between work and rest. He did not design us to be like machines, always working. We are human beings with a built-in need to rest, and by hallowing the Sabbath God gives us permission to meet our need for restoration by having a day of rest.

Indeed, there is something even more wonderful for us to discover here. The crown of all God's creative acts was that of humankind, which took place on day six. Since God rested on the next day, the seventh day, it means that the first day for humankind was a day of rest. That is how we began in the natural order of things, and that is why we speak about working *from* a place of rest. Rest is our starting point. We do not work *into* rest, toiling first and then receiving rest as a reward. We begin with the gift of a day of rest and, because we are rested, we can enter into another period of labour. This is the divine order of creation, the rhythm of grace.

So vital is the Sabbath to our well-being that God has placed it within the Decalogue, the ten basic commands for the ordering and happiness of human society, which express his love and wisdom.

Remember the Sabbath day by keeping it holy. Six days you shall labour and do all your work, but the seventh day is a Sabbath to the Lord your God. On it you shall not do any work, neither you, nor your son or daughter, nor your manservant or maidservant, nor your animals, nor the alien within your gates. For in six days the Lord made the heavens and the earth, the sea, and all that is in them, but he rested on the seventh day. Therefore the Lord blessed the Sabbath day and made it holy. (Exodus 20:8–11)

Keeping the Sabbath is not to be seen as an optional extra for the religious few but as a basic ingredient of a godly life. It is as important as any other of the commandments and should not be ignored, downplayed or treated as irrelevant. It is an abiding principle.

Perhaps our hesitancy about the Sabbath has to do with how we perceive the attitude of Jesus towards this special day. Because Jesus clashed with the Pharisees so fiercely over the practice of Sabbath (see Luke 6:1–11, for example), it is easy to think that he was opposed to it, but that is not the case. It was the cruel abuse of the Sabbath that he corrected, not its proper use, which by his own example he affirmed (see Luke 4:16, for example). When he declared himself to be Lord of the Sabbath (6:5) he was presenting himself as the guardian and interpreter of the Sabbath, not the abolisher of it; and when he pronounced that 'the Sabbath was made for man, not man for the Sabbath' (Mark 2:27), he was reminding us that it is a gift from God for our well-being. It is a universal principle, established for the blessing of all, a day of freedom and not legalistic bondage.

Some may also have the impression that the apostle Paul was opposed to the Sabbath. Certainly he speaks out against the empty religious observance of special days (Colossians 2:16) or of making them a cause for division (Romans 14:5–6), but nowhere does he suggest that the fourth commandment is now obsolete. The early Church seems to have made a natural transition from the Jewish custom of worship on the Sabbath to worship on the first day of the week (Acts 20:7; 1 Corinthians 16:2). The Lord's Day was the natural fulfilment of the Sabbath, and the essential aspects of Sabbath were carried over and integrated into the celebration of the resurrection (Revelation 1:10). When Constantine formalised Sunday as a day of rest in AD321, he was merely recognising the existing Christian custom.

So what does it mean to practise Sabbath in the context of the 21st century? One person who has written extensively on the topic is the theologian Marva J. Dawn. It was her own discovery of the helpfulness of the Sabbath in the midst of her busy life as a teacher, educator and scholar that prompted her to major on this area of Christian formation. 'One of the greatest gifts for my life as one who serves God is observing the Sabbath… Learning to keep an entire day as a Sabbath changed my life,' she says.[13] Dawn emphasises the positive nature of the Sabbath, showing us the benefits of this ancient discipline for the contemporary world. For those of us who have experienced only a negative Sabbath (with endless prohibitions telling us what we couldn't do), her writings provide a refreshing reminder of the delight that can be found in such a day. In trying to grasp what Sabbath may mean for us, we can do no better than to follow the main points of her teaching.[14]

According to Dawn, Sabbath is first about *ceasing.* The word 'sabbath' means to stop, to cease, to desist. Essentially we are freed on this one day of the week from the need to work, to produce, to accomplish and achieve. We are allowed to stop and are able to bask in our acceptance by God for who we are, not what we do. It is an opportunity for us to rest in the sovereignty of God, express our trust in God for our needs and be released from the worry and anxiety that go along with our vain attempts to run our own lives. This means, of course, choosing to live counterculturally, for the world around us treats Sunday as just another day. When we choose not to work, buy or sell, we are setting ourselves free from the acquisitiveness of the world in which we live.

Second, Sabbath is about *resting*. This is not another word for idleness but means a constructive resting that is centred upon God. The foundation for this is the spiritual rest that is the fruit of being secure in the grace of God, knowing that we are loved and that God is at work in us to accomplish all he asks of us. The purpose of worship is to bring us to a deeper realisation of who we are, and all that we have, in Christ. Physical rest is possible because we have this deep-seated peace of God in our hearts, and our bodies can therefore relax. We can have time to sleep, to walk, to exercise, to do the things that refresh our bodies. Closely allied with this is the emotional rest that comes as we slow down, focus our minds on God and allow ourselves to unwind. Our careworn souls are rejuvenated as we concentrate on God's care for us, and healing takes place as we remember that he is Lord. Even our minds can be rested as we cease trying to fathom everything and solve every problem. Exposing ourselves more intentionally to the word of God renews our minds and helps us gain a truer perspective on things.

Third, Sabbath is about *embracing*, about taking hold afresh of the values of the gospel and applying them to our lives. It gives us a reminder that we are God's people and that we are called to live distinctive lives as representatives of the kingdom of God. This is one reason why meeting together with others is integral to a Sabbath way of life. In choosing to practise Sabbath, we are expressing a certain attitude towards time (that it belongs to God), and demonstrating that having time for people is important to us. It is a day that has always been associated with giving and with generosity, too (see again 1 Corinthians 16:2), so we are encouraged to move from wanting even more stuff to a simplicity of life.

Perhaps the most challenging part of this aspect of Sabbath is that we are given the opportunity to embrace our calling again. We are given the time to review what we are doing, listen to God again for his direction, wait in his presence to be strengthened and offer ourselves anew to his service in the world.

Finally, Sabbath is about *feasting* or celebrating. It should be a day that includes fun and festivity, for these are some of the ways in which we can restore our souls. Again, worship is part of this, for worship should help us to rejoice in God and to gladden our hearts as we do so. The day can be filled with good music, with the enjoyment of beauty, with the fellowship that comes through a shared meal and time to talk with one another. It is not a day for sadness but for gladness, when we experience the *shalom* of God— the sense of wholeness and well-being that is found when our lives are in harmony with God.

The greatest danger in restoring Sabbath to our lives is that we are led back into legalism and the kind of bondage that lays down rules and regulations about what we should or should not do. This is not my intention at all, nor that of any of the growing number of contemporary writers about Sabbath that I have read.[15] It is really for individuals to work out for themselves how best to maintain a day of rest, and to know what will most effectively restore their souls, even if it has to be on a day other than Sunday.

The point is that God has commanded us to set aside one day for rest and remembrance of all that he has done for us. Only when we acknowledge it as a direct command from God will we develop the kind of inner conviction that enables us to break free of unhealthy patterns of living and working, and the stranglehold that our 24/7 society has on our thinking . Only when we see it as God's gracious invitation to spend time with him will we be motivated enough to leave aside the many alternative demands on our time in order to be with the true lover of our souls.

We do well to remind ourselves of the special blessings that come when we re-establish Sabbath as part of the pattern of our lives. Isaiah tells us, for example:

If you keep your feet from breaking the Sabbath and from doing as you please on my holy day, if you call the Sabbath a delight and the Lord's holy day honourable, and if you honour it by not going your own way and not doing as you please or speaking idle words, then you will find your joy in the Lord, and I will cause you to ride on the heights of the land and to feast on the inheritance of your father Jacob. (Isaiah 58:13–14)

Once we have adopted a Sabbath way of living and built the discipline of a day of rest into our lives, it becomes natural to enjoy Sabbath moments, too. This is why Jesus could sit and rest by the well. It was a reflection of his being centred upon God and the fact that he was at rest within himself as a result.

9

Busy doing nothing

The sign outside the church made a bold proclamation: 'God never goes on holiday.' I think I know the message that it was meant to put across (that his care over us is not interrupted while he takes an annual two-week vacation) but to me it conveyed something else—the sense that God is slightly disapproving of those who do go on holiday. Surely the truth is that God actually does go on holiday, for he is with us as much in our vacation time as in our working time. In fact, we are more likely to discover his presence when we are rested and relaxed than when we are busy and preoccupied in our normal frenzied routines.

My encounter with the sign helped me to recognise that, as Christians, we have a strong theology of work but virtually no theology of leisure, and yet both are important in healthy living. Much is written about being a Christian at work, and about the virtues of hard work and honouring God by the way we do our work, but what about when we are not at work? How do we use our time outside office hours? Should we even have time for ourselves? What do we do when we are not saving the world?

Christians are very ambivalent when it comes to leisure. There seems to be a deep-seated fear of wasting time, an aversion to anything that is not directly productive or spiritual. There is a suspicion that enjoying leisure means giving way to the 'flesh', that somehow it is 'worldly' and may lead us into sin. We have so many noble tasks to do that amusing ourselves is not high on our list of priorities, and we may even feel that it is shameful to spend time on ourselves rather than on the cause we serve. Hobbies are seen as 'diversions', not only stealing our time but also leading us away from being fully committed to God. Pastimes are regarded as irrelevant, the choice of those who have nothing better to do. Those who work in countries where survival is all that matters may even feel that leisure is obscene, a luxury of Western affluence. No wonder we struggle to take a day off and feel guilty when we find ourselves with time on our hands.

By sitting at the well for a few minutes, doing nothing, Jesus was actually enjoying a moment or two of leisure, and by his example he grants us permission to build time for leisure into our overworked lives. The thought of leisure is also implicit in the practice of the Sabbath, when we are given permission to cease from our work. Indeed, knowing how to use such a day well is one of the challenges of our acceptance of its importance, and leisure is surely a valid ingredient in the construction of a day of rest. It cannot just be about church worship services. Theologian Robert Lee points to the significance of human life itself, and notes, 'It suggests that life's fulfilment is not be identified completely with work, but that leisure (or rest) is an indispensable ingredient in the rhythm of work and rest and worship.'[16] He quotes Alan Richardson: 'Man's work, like his Creator's, is crowned with his rest, and his chief end is not to labour but to enjoy God forever.'[17]

Christian tradition has often linked contemplation with leisure, and one translation of the Vulgate (Latin) version of Psalm 46:10 expresses it like this: 'Be at leisure and see that I am God.' I know from my own experience that when I slow down and am most fully relaxed, it is easier to be aware of God and respond to his promptings. To be at leisure from myself and my preoccupations, even for a short while, can open the doorway to God's presence. Far from leading us away from God, leisure can draw us towards God by bringing us to a state where our spirits are more sensitive to his voice. Further, when we practise leisure, we care for ourselves and, by so doing, ensure that we are able to keep on caring for others. Graham Neville, in his book *Free Time*, calls this the 'third love' in the summing up of the law: 'Worship expresses love of

God. The active life is where we show our love for our neighbour. We love ourselves in leisure.'[18]

Leisure from a Christian perspective has to do with enjoying God and his creation. It is about being at home in the world he has made, appreciating its wonder and enjoying its attractions. It expresses a God-directed attitude towards our work (important but not the 'be all and end all') and the way we use our time (a gift of his grace), and is one of the pleasurable means by which we refresh and renew ourselves for further activity. Leisure is morally neutral. We have to decide for ourselves what constitutes legitimate leisure and how much leisure is appropriate.

The Western world has, of course, gone overboard on leisure. We have made a very profitable industry out of it, and most regard leisure as their right rather than as a gift. Indeed, for many, the pursuit of leisure is an end in itself, the main goal in life, while work is but a necessary interruption supporting the main object-ive, which is having a good time. People live for the weekend, when they can enjoy their free time and really let themselves go. This hedonistic approach to life is not what I am advocating here. Likewise, I am conscious that while some have too much leisure, and don't know what to do with their time, others have neither enough leisure nor enough free time. It is for this second group that I am writing—those who say, 'Spare time? What spare time?'—in order to encourage them that it is both permissible and essential to create space in their lives for leisure. Even if we feel we don't need it, we should incorporate it as a spiritual discipline.

Our word 'leisure' has its origin in the Latin verb *licere*, which means to be permitted or to be free. Simply stated, leisure is free time. It is discretionary time when we can decide for ourselves what to do, when we are free from the more obvious and formal duties that a paid job or other social responsibilities require of us. Work is that by which we make a living. Duty is that which social life imposes on us. Leisure is that which we choose to do beyond the limits of work and duty, and is undertaken for our own pleasure and satisfaction. In this sense, leisure is about freedom—what we choose to do because we want to rather than because necessity requires us to do it.

From another perspective, leisure is an attitude, a state of mind, a condition of the soul. It is about feeling at ease, being calm, becoming relaxed. It provides the opportunity for reflection and for activities that enrich the mind, strengthen the body, restore the soul and renew the spirit. Leisure has to do with learning and is undertaken for the purpose of the development of our whole being. It can lead to self-discovery, creativity and the seeing of new possibilities.

Leisure is also about rest and recuperation. Leisure activities are those that put back into us what the day has taken out. They are ways by which we receive 'input' for ourselves to balance up the 'output' that work and other responsibilities require of us. As such, they are permitted because they are good for us: they give to us rather than steal from us. The range of things that come under the heading of leisure is vast, and such activities are individually chosen. What they have in common is that they give energy to us and revitalise us. Understood in this way, leisure is not a luxury or even an optional extra, but a necessity. Those of us who are most busy are most in need of restorative leisure.

We can think about leisure under three headings: relaxation, recreation and play.

Relaxation refers to those leisure activities that most help us to re-energise. We need relaxation when our energy is at its lowest and we do not feel like doing much. Such activities are likely to be passive in nature, when we are receiving rather than giving and nothing is expected of us. John Chrysostom, the 'golden mouthed' preacher of the fourth-century church, reputedly said, 'The bow that is seldom unstrung will quickly break.' We are designed to operate under pressure but not to live under it all the time. If we do, we are likely to crack, like the bow that is always under tension. In the rhythm of work and rest, we must be sure to relax.

Relaxation might include such things as sleeping, soaking in the bath, watching a film or reading a novel.

Recreation becomes possible as we recover our energy. It involves the investment of some energy in order that we may be re-energised even further. The link between recreation and the re-creation of our souls is obvious. It is as we enjoy recreation that we are recharged. Recreation is thus active in nature. It may involve such things as sport, making music, walking, cycling, jogging, gardening, fishing and so on. These activities can be done alone or with others, depending on the needs of our personality type. Hobbies are a form of recreation. They take us out of ourselves and our thoughts, allowing us to focus on something else for a while. As we become absorbed in our hobby, and without realising it, our minds, emotions and bodies are being renewed. We can return to our work refreshed and invigorated.

The third aspect of leisure is play. This is light-hearted fun and can actually occur only when we are well rested. Indeed, we could say that fun and laughter, the hallmarks of play, are a sign that we are in good shape. When we are overstretched and under pressure, we become intense and serious. The first thing to go is our light-heartedness. Only when we are back to normal can we smile, enjoy a joke and become playful again. Theologian and social reformer Walter Rauschenbusch said:

The real joy of life is its play. Play is anything we do for the joy and love of doing it, apart from any profit, compulsion, or sense of duty. It is the real living of life with the feeling of freedom and self-expression. Play is the business of childhood, and its continuation in later years is the prolongation of youth. Real civilisation should increase the margin of time given to play. [19]

Playful activities may include games (board games, party games, computer games), picnics, meals with friends, non-competitive sports, simply hanging out together and so on.

I have suggested that Christians often have an underdeveloped or negative attitude towards leisure, and, while this is often the case, we should remember that in one sense the Church is the mother of leisure. In medieval times, holy days consisted of the five major feasts of Mary, the days of the apostles and a great number of saints' days. Added to this were many other days commemorating patron saints. These holy days gave even the poorest people time to rest and celebrate, and became the forerunner of holidays as we know them now. Far from being opposed to holidays, I believe that God is in favour of them, and I regularly encourage busy Christian workers to make sure that they plan time for holidays into their schedule.

Holidays allow for all three of the component parts of leisure that we have mentioned—relaxation, recreation and playfulness—to be enjoyed together, and are major sources of rejuvenation. I always suggest that people have at least one holiday of two weeks each year. In the first week, we restore energy that has been given out previously. During the second week, we store energy for future demands. This is why an annual break of a fortnight is actually better than two breaks of one week each. Medical doctor and missionary adviser Ruth Fowke says, 'Leisure is a necessary ingredient for health and a command from God. The Biblical principle is short restorative breaks, preferably daily, and regular, longer interludes from obligations.'[20]

The Bishop of Reading, Stephen Cottrell, created a stir a few years ago when he handed out egg timers to commuters at his local railway station, with the encouragement to spend at least three minutes each day learning 'the joyful art of doing nothing'.[21] It was his way of urging people to detox themselves from the busyness of life and discover what happens when we stop and rest, ditch our endless 'to do' lists, resist the constant stream of emails and challenge our 24/7 culture.

'I want to celebrate what happens when we dare to stop and reconnect with a hiddenness inside ourselves where rest and play issue forth in all sorts of wild, unexpected and creative ways,' he writes. Stopping, and doing nothing very much, is a good thing to do: when we do it, we find that we rediscover ourselves very slowly in relation to others and the world itself. From his own experience Bishop Stephen shares, 'Not only do I become more myself—and that is joy enough—but from myself there comes fruitfulness.'[22]

Reflection

- How can you practise the discipline of stopping?
  - Are there any still points in your day, where you can stop for a few minutes?
  - Can you make room for a stopover, a morning/afternoon/evening for reflection and quiet space?
  - What about a grinding halt—a few days for retreat or a holiday?

- What might a Sabbath way of life look like for you? What objections to the Sabbath do you find in your own heart? What difficulties might you encounter as you seek to incorporate this discipline? What might spur you on to establish it as a helpful routine?

- What part does leisure play in your life? What resistance to it do you find within yourself?
  - What do you currently do for relaxation?
  - For recreation?
  - For fun?

It's important to drink and be refreshed on the journey

10

The gift

We have concentrated so far on the example of Jesus, watching him sit by the well and rest. As we have pondered this simple scene from his life, we have reflected on the similarities with our own lives. We have recognised that we too are on a journey, that often we feel tired and that we need to build into our busy schedules periods of rest. Now, as the story unfolds, we give our attention to the teaching of Jesus and eavesdrop on the dialogue between him and the Samaritan woman.

We have no indication of how long Jesus had been sitting alone by the well. Presently, however, a woman approaches from the village to draw water. It is an unusual occurrence, for it is already midday and the sun is at its hottest. Women normally drew water in the cool of the early morning, when the well would be a hive of activity. A lone woman approaching at midday is unexpected. No doubt she too is surprised to see a man at the well, and she probably hesitates as she draws near, for she can see he is a stranger, and a Jew at that.

Jesus is the first to speak, and his need for refreshment causes him to request a favour. 'Will you give me a drink?' he asks (John 4:7). The woman is taken aback, for she is not expecting to be in conversation with anyone, let alone a Jewish man. She has come at this unpopular time deliberately, to avoid meeting others. There is an edge to her reply, for she is uncomfortable. Recognising the cultural divide between them, she replies sharply. 'You are a Jew and I am a Samaritan woman. How can you ask me for a drink?' (v. 9). There is little compassion in her voice, little desire to help a stranger. Jesus, however, responds with a statement that lifts the conversation out of the mundane and beyond issues of culture and gender, into the spiritual realm. 'If you knew the gift of God and who it is that asks you for a drink, you would have asked him and he would have given you living water' (v. 10).

This is a crucial statement for our understanding of all that follows in this encounter, and one that sheds considerable light on what it means to work from a place of rest. In speaking about the gift of God, Jesus introduces us to the whole notion of grace. Grace is the beautiful word that speaks of the merciful action of God towards needy men and women, giving us what we could never earn and doing for us what we could never achieve by ourselves. The whole of the Christian life is based upon this continuing movement of God towards us, undeserved as it is. He is always the one making the first move, reaching out to us in love. All that is required is that we respond to this prior movement in faith and with obedience. We don't have to start it. Nor do we have to keep it going. From first to last, the Christian life is lived on the basis of grace. Everything comes to us as gift, and by the initiative of God.

But what exactly is the gift of God? This would surely have been the woman's question, and it may be ours, too. In the ancient Near East, water was such a precious commodity that it was sometimes called 'the gift of God', but here Jesus is speaking about something even more precious. The answer is that he himself is the gift of God. The gracious movement of God towards a needy world comes to us wrapped up in a person. John has already made this wonderful statement: 'For God so loved the world that he *gave* his one and only Son' (3:16, italics mine). Paul recognised the same truth with his bold exclamation, 'Thanks be to God for his indescribable gift!' (2 Corinthians 9:15).

The gift of God finds its visible expression in Christ's coming to earth, living our life and then offering himself as an atoning sacrifice for our sins. In doing this, he made it possible for us to be forgiven, to come back into a relationship with God and to receive eternal life. He did for us what we could never do for ourselves, and he did it even though we did not deserve such kindness. This is why salvation is a gift. 'For it is by grace you have been saved, through faith—and this not from yourselves, it is the gift of God—not by works, so that no one can boast' (Ephesians 2:8–9).

We relate to God on the basis of grace. This is how we begin the Christian life and it is how we are to continue it. 'So then, just as you received Christ Jesus as Lord, continue to live in him, rooted and built up in him' (Colossians 2:6–7). We are to live this new life not by trying hard or doing our best but in dependency upon him, receiving all that we need as gift and trusting that God will enable us to do everything that he asks of us. We are to be like trees, rooting ourselves in the good soil of his life, drawing all the sustenance we need from our relationship with him and refusing to depend upon our own strength. We are to be like buildings, resting on the solid foundation of his finished work rather than the shaky ground of our own accomplishments.

So far, as we have explored what it means to work from a place of rest, we have emphasised the gift of physical rest, but now we begin to see that it involves a spiritual rest as well. Indeed, we can say that this is the heart of the matter. To work from a place of rest means recognising that anything we do must be done in response to the prior working of God within us. We seek to avoid doing things for God, well-intentioned as we may be, but choose rather to allow God to work through us. We do not strive or strain to accomplish things on his behalf through self-effort, but wait for him to move within us and direct us into what he wants to accomplish. Then we respond in faith and obedience to whatever opens up before us. As we do this, we discover that his yoke is easy and his burden is light (see Matthew 11:28–30).

I think this is what we see happening at the well of Sychar. Jesus is using these spare moments to commune with the Father, enjoy his fellowship and listen for any revelation of his will (see John 5:19, 30; 8:28; 12:49 and 14:10 to recognise this as the pattern of his life). When the Samaritan woman approaches, he begins to recognise that the Father is at work in this encounter. This is not a chance meeting but a divinely planned coming-together. The genuine expression of his need opens the door to the conversation. It is not some contrived and artificial 'ice-breaker' but a genuine request. As soon as the woman starts to speak, Jesus recognises her deep need and he addresses it. Everything happens normally and naturally; there is no striving to make something happen, only a sense of realisation that God is at work and responding accordingly.

Here we have a wonderful example of collaboration. The word means literally 'to labour together with another', and this is how Christian ministry is meant to be. It is, as we have said already, a partnership, with God as the senior partner. He initiates and we respond. We can relax because we do not have to make things happen. 'For we are God's fellow workers,' says Paul (1 Corinthians 3:9). We are able to love others because we have first received the love of God ourselves. We operate on the basis of overflow, receiving for ourselves and then giving out to others from the abundance given to us (see 1 John 4:19).

In a very real sense, this way of working is pictured for us in the Hebrew concept of time, where there is 'evening and morning' rather than the other way around. Eugene Petersen explains its significance:

[This] Hebrew evening/morning sequence conditions us to the rhythms of grace. We go to sleep, and God begins his work. As we sleep he develops his covenant. We wake and are called out to participate in God's creative action. We respond in faith, in work. But always grace is previous and primary. We wake into a world we didn't make, into a salvation we didn't earn. Evening: God begins, without our help, his creative day. Morning: God calls us to enjoy and share and develop the work he initiated.[23]

It can also be seen in the fulfilment of the Sabbath as described in Hebrews 4, where the writer speaks of a 'rest' that is still to be experienced: 'There remains, then, a Sabbath-rest for the people of God; for anyone who enters God's rest also rests from his own work, just as God did from his' (vv. 9–10). The physical benefits of keeping Sabbath have already been noted, but here we see the deeper spiritual dimension behind it. The Christian life is not meant to be lived out of natural strength or self-effort but through allowing God to be powerfully at work within us: 'And I will put my Spirit in you and *move you* to follow my decrees and be careful to keep my laws' (Ezekiel 36:27, italics mine). We can live in a relaxed and easy way because we are no longer depending on ourselves. Thus the 'rest of God' mentioned in Hebrews does not refer to the blessedness of heaven but to the calmness we experience as we lean heavily upon the grace of God. We know that even our ability to serve God comes to us as a gift.

. There are many other scriptures that underline this truth for us, and it is a truth that Paul emphasises time and again. This was his personal understanding, summed up in Galatians 2:20: 'I have been crucified with Christ and I no longer live, but Christ lives in me.' This has sometimes been called the 'exchanged life', for it involved Paul in coming to the end of his proud, self-righteous approach as a Pharisee and surrendering himself to the life of God within him. He was well aware that he could take no credit for anything that God did through him, because everything was dependent upon grace: 'By the grace of God I am what I am, and his grace towards me was not without effect. No, I worked harder than all of them—yet not I, but the grace of God that was with me' (1 Corinthians 15:10). He did not trust in his powerful personality, intellectual ability or religious zeal as he sought to proclaim Christ. 'To this end I labour,' he wrote, 'struggling with all *his energy*, which so powerfully works in me' (Colossians 1:29, italics mine).

Paul enthusiastically commended this truth to others. To encourage the Philippians, he writes, 'Continue to work out your salvation with fear and trembling, for it is God who works in you to will and to act according to his good purpose' (Philippians 2:12–13). He reminds the Thessalonians that their confidence should be in God: 'The one who calls you is faithful and he will do it' (1 Thessalonians 5:24). He commends the Ephesians to a God who is 'able to do immeasurably more than all we ask or imagine, according to his power that is at work within us' (Ephesians 3:20). Time and again he says the same thing: don't strive to make things happen; relax and let God work through you.

One well-known Christian leader who discovered this truth for himself is Richard Foster. He writes:

When I was fresh out of seminary in my first church pastorate, I encountered deeply needy people—and quickly discovered that I was one of them. They were parched for the living water of spiritual substance. But when I tried to lead them to it by enthusiasm and self-effort, I found that my own resources quickly ran dry. I needed help in moving to a deeper level of life with God, for myself and our faith community.[24]

Foster's search led him to study the lives of many of the great men and women of faith, and he found that what they had in common was an intimate awareness of God in every minute and every circumstance of their lives. He began to practise some of the classic spiritual disciplines and to discover the grace of God at work within him, letting go of what he calls the dry husks of self-effort. 'It is impossible to take on the light yoke of Jesus,' he concludes, 'if we are already strapped into the weighty harness of self-effort and willpower.'[25]

It should be clear by now that when we speak of working from a place of rest, we are not talking about being idle or lazy, or even passive. We are talking about a different way of working altogether. We do work hard and we have periods of intense busyness, but our work is not the frantic effort that originates from an independent self, vainly trying to prove its own worth through its achievements. Rather it is the steady, relaxed working that springs from a relationship with God in which he has become the source of our life. This is the way of working that Jesus models and graciously points us towards.

11

Living water

We continue to eavesdrop on the conversation at the well. The dialogue appears to be taking place on two levels, with Jesus using natural things to talk about spiritual issues, but the Samaritan woman taking everything literally and getting more and more confused. Skilfully, and with great care, Jesus begins to expose the deepest needs of her heart and to tell her where true satisfaction can be found.

From asking for a drink of water for himself, Jesus moves on to offering 'living' water to the woman (John 4:10). He, of course, is referring to something spiritual, but she can only see it in terms of 'flowing' water, thinking of fresh water as opposed to that which is still and possibly stagnant. She is puzzled over how he can find such water at the well. This leads Jesus to elucidate his meaning further. He is offering something far more satisfying than the quenching of physical thirst. Anyone who drinks natural water will eventually thirst again, but he wants to give a kind of water that will satisfy the deepest needs of the human soul, and do so permanently. He is, in fact, offering her the gift of eternal life.

We were created in the image of God and made to know him in a personal way. When that relationship is missing from our lives, our souls are dissatisfied. We become parched and thirsty on the inside and a longing to find something to satisfy our emptiness grows within us. Everyone suffers from this soul thirst, although we may not recognise it or acknowledge it as a spiritual issue. We have many ways of slaking our thirst, too. Consumerism is one common attempt to meet the longing of our hearts. Buying things offers a temporary satisfaction as we are thrilled with our latest acquisition, but, once the novelty wears off, we start the search all over again for the 'next thing' we must have. Some people fill the vacuum with pleasure seeking, with exciting leisure pursuits and exotic holidays. For a while, these diversions quench our thirst, but, once they are over and normality returns, so does the emptiness. Others get their buzz from sport, from drugs, from sexual adventures, even from working hard and achieving success. They provide a passing relief but always, in the cold light of day, when reality returns, the deep dissatisfaction surfaces once more.

It was to meet this need that Jesus came. He is both the gift and the giver, since he is the answer to our need and the one who offers to meet that need. What he has to give to us is 'living water' or, as we might say, the water of life. 'I am come that they may have life, and have it to the full,' are his words (John 10:10). We have only to ask and he will give to us this wonderful life. It is not just a quantity of life (continuing beyond the grave) but a quality of life (to be enjoyed here and now), and it is guaranteed to satisfy the longing of our soul because it is the very life of God.

The Bible uses two Greek words for life. The first, *bios*, refers to natural life, from which we get our word 'biology'. Everyone who is alive has this *bios* kind of life. The second word is *zoe*, which refers to spiritual life, or the life of God. This is the missing ingredient in human hearts. It was there before the Fall, but when sin came into the world we 'died'—that is, we lost the *zoe* life of God and became spiritually dead. In offering us the water of life, Jesus wants to revive us and fill us with the *zoe* life of God.

This offer of life constitutes the heart of the gospel invitation. Isaiah put it like this: 'Come, all you who are thirsty, come to the waters; and you who have no money, come, buy and eat! Come, buy wine and milk without money and without cost' (55:1). It is available to all, and in good measure, and it comes freely as the gift of grace. The book of Revelation also speaks of God's marvellous offer: 'To him who is thirsty I will give to drink without cost from the spring of the water of life' (21:6), and again, 'Whoever is thirsty, let him come; and whoever wishes, let him take the free gift of the water of life' (22:17). Jesus repeated his own invitation at the feast of Tabernacles: 'If anyone is thirsty, let him come to me and drink. Whoever believes in me, as the Scripture has said, streams of living water will flow from within him' (John 7:37–38).

When we come by faith to Christ, we begin to drink this living water and to receive the life of God in our spirit. It erupts or 'wells up' (John 4:14) from deep within us, like a spring bursting from the ground, animating us with all the regenerating power of God. It is planted inside us like a tiny seed that begins to germinate and grow, changing and transforming us into the likeness of Christ. Indeed, the *zoe* life of God is the same as the resurrection life of Christ, just as it is the same as the creative life of the Spirit, and it releases tremendous spiritual energy into our innermost beings. We should never underestimate what happens to us at conversion. Indeed, we should seek to know more of the amazing power that is available to us, which wants to operate through us.

In working from a place of rest, it is this powerful life within us that we are seeking to release. Jesus promised that streams of living (life-giving) water would flow from within us, and, as we learn to depend upon him, this is exactly what we can expect to happen. We step aside in order that Christ may come flowing through. Richard Foster puts it like this: 'If I am to enter into the eternal, uncreated life that originates in God alone, I must surrender my life. When I enter the with-God life, it is not my life any more; it is Christ's life, in which I am privileged to become a participant.'[26]

Having heard Jesus speak of a kind of water that can quench the thirst permanently, the Samaritan woman sees the potential for saving herself some hard work. Perhaps playfully, she suggests that she would not need to keep coming to the well if she had the living water of which he speaks. Humour, like sarcasm and cynicism, is so often used as a shield against the truth, isn't it? This woman is skilled in deflecting anything that gets too close to her real need. Jesus, however, surprises her by changing the topic of conversation completely, asking her to call her husband. Flustered and embarrassed, she denies any such relationship. Then, with the kind of insight reserved for prophets, Jesus reveals the truth of her situation: she has had five such relationships already, and even now is in a relationship with a man who is not her husband. Her soul is laid bare before this stranger who seems to know everything about her.

We wonder about the woman's life story. What has happened in her past to make her the person she is? Why is she isolated from the other women of the village? What pain has she known, what rejection has she felt? How does she perceive herself and how do others regard her? Is she a victim of abuse, the exploited plaything of powerful men? Or has she chosen her own course in life, using her sexuality to manipulate others, gaining what she wants with little sense of shame or guilt? One thing is sure: Jesus does not condemn or judge her. He brings her to realise her sense of need by speaking the truth clearly, not to humiliate but to help and rescue her.

It seems probable that her lifestyle reflected the thirst within her own soul for love. The need to be accepted and approved by others is one of the deepest needs in the human heart, and we all feel its pull. The craving for intimacy and connection is one of the most powerful motivators of human behaviour. We assume that this need can be met through other people, and often we form relationships in the hope that we will find the love we crave. We do our best to make ourselves attractive and presentable so that others will like us, yet deep down we know that human love is never enough to satisfy us. The best of relationships leave us unfulfilled, while the ones that break down confirm our worst fears. We feel unloved, and wonder if we are lovable at all.

This thirst for love is, in fact, a symptom of our thirst for God and for the love that only he can give. God is love and we were made to rest in his love, finding our identity and security in the knowledge that we are his beloved ones. Again, the Fall robbed us of that innate sense of identity, so we come into the world searching for love and, sadly, looking in all the wrong places. Only when we come to Jesus and begin to drink of the living water that he alone can give do we begin to understand that we are loved by God, and that his love for us is unconditional and unchanging. The more we read the scriptures and open ourselves to the Spirit, the more this wonderful truth sinks into our hearts and gradually shapes how we define ourselves. We come to believe that we are indeed God's beloved children (Ephesians 5:1) and that nothing can rob us of our true identity (Romans 8:38–39).

Liberated from our feelings of unworthiness and fear of rejection, we begin to live securely in God's love. We are no longer prisoners to the approval of others, no longer dependent on the fix of human affirmation and praise. Of course it is good to be loved by others and it is helpful to be affirmed by them, but we no longer need these things to make us feel worthwhile. We carry a sense of worth and value within ourselves because we know we are loved by God. This frees us to give love to others because we know ourselves to be loved. Not surprisingly, the more we give love, the more we receive it.

What has this to do with working from a place of rest? If our need for love and approval is not met in God, it can easily find expression through our work. We can find ourselves working hard to achieve success so that we feel better about ourselves, and to gain approval from others. We can find ourselves unable to establish healthy boundaries in our lives because we are afraid to say 'No', so we end up taking on more and more responsibilities. What is more, our need to be loved can manifest itself in unhealthy patterns of relating, helping others because we have a need inside us to be needed—that is, loved. We drive ourselves to the limit and work ourselves to the bone because of the reward we get—a feeling that we are loved, accepted and worthwhile *because of what we do*. This means that we are living out of an emotional deficit, making up for our inner lack through external activities.

Such behaviour can appear very spiritual and noble and can easily masquerade as Christian ministry, but it is not, and it is dangerous. Christian ministry is the outflow of the life of God, the release of love through the lives of those who know themselves to be loved by God. Thus it is relaxed, natural, easy and, above all, sustainable. When we are working to gain love, we can never stop. We become driven, uptight and anxious. This is the way to exhaustion and eventually burn-out.

Those of us in Christian ministry must know how to drink deeply of the living water and find our soul thirst continually satisfied in Christ. In particular, we must allow our need for love and approval to be satisfied in him. This is why, in the definition of 'stopping' in Chapter 7, we saw that first we must pause and remember who we are—God's beloved children. We cannot hear this truth too many times, and we cannot remind ourselves of it too often. In the challenges of life, we easily forget who we really are, and we fall back into our old ways of looking for love through what we do. We need to come often to the well and drink, allowing the love of God to fill every part of our being and refresh our parched and weary souls.

12

Drinking from the well

To the Samaritans, the well at Sychar was much more than a place to find water. It was a site of great historical importance and something of a cultural icon, for it connected them to their past. They were proud of this well, with its reminder of their sacred history, for the patriarch Jacob ('our father', John 4:12) had been there to water his flocks and had drunk its refreshing water himself.

Archaeologists are uncertain as to whether Sychar was, in fact, the biblical town of Shechem, but there is no uncertainty over the location of the famous well. It is generally agreed that it is to be found near to the modern-day town of Nablus, and can still be seen today. Originally the well is thought to have been over 23 metres deep, with a diameter at the top of 3 metres. The plot of ground where it stood had been given to Joseph by his father Jacob, and Joseph was buried nearby, so it had a long and significant history (see Genesis 33:18–19; Joshua 24:32). We can sense the woman's pride in her people's ancestry as she delivers a brief history lesson to the Jewish stranger.

Throughout the world, and especially in developing countries, wells are vitally important in maintaining life, as anyone involved in development work will testify. Those of us who are accustomed to having water on tap can easily take the supply of safe drinking water for granted, but it is not so in many places, and certainly in ancient times a source of good drinking water really was a gift from God. The finding of water and the digging of wells appear to have been constant necessities in Old Testament times. Not surprisingly, wells in the Bible are symbols of spiritual refreshment and renewal. As the prophet Isaiah wrote, 'With joy you will draw water from the wells of salvation' (Isaiah 12:3).

For anyone intent on pursuing a spiritual journey with God, the ability to refresh one's soul is essential. We must be able to draw on the life of God for ourselves and not be dependent upon others providing refreshment for us. It is not enough for us to sit on the edge of the well, looking admiringly at the water below. We have to draw water for ourselves and then drink it. However, there is an increasing tendency nowadays for believers to adopt a 'consumer' mentality when it comes to maintaining their inner lives. Too easily we see our churches and the programmes they offer as being the source of our life in God. We expect preachers and teachers to provide the water of life for us and never develop the ability to care for our own souls.

So much excellent material is available to us nowadays, in the form of books, DVDs, podcasts and online transmissions, that we don't necessarily have to do anything ourselves. We can hear the best preachers any time, anywhere, through the internet, and we are not required to exert ourselves at all. While, from the perspective of those isolated and lacking in fellowship, this is a great provision, from another perspective it can make us extremely lazy, meaning that we never develop the personal capacity to draw from the well of life that God has provided for us in Christ. This lack of personal engagement means that we can easily deceive ourselves into thinking that we are growing spiritually when we are simply increasing our head knowledge. Spiritual growth comes through revelation, and that requires us to play an active part in the process of spiritual formation. Of course, this requires not only effort but also time, and that is what many of us lack. The temptation to take short cuts, and to live off the revelation of others, is very real.

In 2007, the Willow Creek Church in America published the findings of some research its members had commissioned concerning their spiritual growth.[27] This was the church that pioneered seeker-sensitive services, and is one of the best-known 'mega churches' in the world. To their surprise, they discovered that people were not growing as well as they expected. Indeed, out of 5000 surveyed, they discovered that 25 per cent described themselves as 'stalled' spiritually, while another ten per cent of the most active people considered themselves 'dissatisfied' with their spiritual lives. The findings were published in a report called *Reveal*, and show the danger of assuming that because people attend church programmes (even of the highest quality) they are therefore going to grow spiritually.

One major finding in the report stood out for me. It was the realisation that while the Church has an important part to play in spiritual formation in the early stages of a person's Christian life, later it becomes less important: what matters then is that individuals develop personal spiritual practices of their own to sustain them on their faith journey. In other words, the greatest gift a church can give to its members is to show them how to access the life of God themselves.

Again, the conversation between Jesus and the women speaks to our situation. Ever the realist, the woman points out a significant flaw in his offer of living water. 'Sir,' she says, 'you have nothing to draw with and the well is deep' (John 4:11). She has brought a water jar with her but Jesus has no such equipment. I used to think that when she left the jar behind on returning to her village (v. 28), it was in a moment of excited absentmindedness, but maybe it was more deliberate than that. Perhaps she realised that Jesus still needed a drink and, therefore, the use of her water jar!

We could use this part of the story as a simple allegory. The well of salvation is indeed extremely deep. Christ has not only brought us into a relationship with the Father, but has also opened up for us a way by which we can begin to receive into our souls the very fullness that is in God. If we are to enjoy the benefits of all that is ours in him and to refresh our souls, we need something to draw the water with, and then we must make sure we drink deeply and thirstily.

The water jar speaks to us of the spiritual practices or disciplines available to us, by which we can receive more of the life of God. They are many and varied, and different ones work for different people. What is more, different practices may be more appropriate at certain times for us than others. We can define a spiritual discipline as 'any action we take that expresses our dependency on God and enables us to live from his divine resources. They are the practical means by which his life is allowed to flow into our lives'.[28]

At first sight, this emphasis on the part we have to play may seem to contradict our earlier assertion that the Christian life is lived on the basis of grace, but, as writer Dallas Willard has frequently pointed out, 'Grace is not opposed to effort, it is opposed to earning.'[29] In fact, by actively seeking more of the life of God, we are simply cooperating with the work of God within us. Indeed, our very desire for God can be understood as his gift, the way in which he draws us closer to himself. He creates the soul thirst within us and then graciously satisfies our longing. One of my most basic prayers, which I pray as often as I can, is 'Lord, make me hungry for you.' When that hunger (or thirst) is there in our souls, we will generally have no difficulty in seeking God and finding practical ways to do so. Left to ourselves, unaided by his grace, none of us would seek after God. Any of us can become distracted and lethargic unless he moves within us.

In my own spiritual journey, I have discovered six disciplines in particular that I find especially important and productive. I place them into two groups. The first set of three are those disciplines that bring us closer to God, and they are particularly relevant in the busy world in which we live. They are stillness, silence and solitude. Together they act as a powerful combination in helping us to slow down, tune in to God and become aware of his presence. The second trio are disciplines that take us deeper with God, moving us from the shallows of life into the depths where we can experience even more of his love and grace. They are reflection, Bible meditation and contemplation, and they help us to consider what God is doing in our lives, receive his truth into the core of our being where it can transform us, and bring us to quiet adoration before the lover of our souls. Of course, I am still growing in my understanding and practice of each of these disciplines, but they are the ones which have had the greatest impact on my own walk with God, and which I unhesitatingly commend to others.

Worship is perhaps not always on the list of spiritual disciplines, but it should be, because it is one of the chief ways by which God shares his life with us. Interestingly, the discussion between Jesus and the woman at the well moves on to the topic of worship. Almost as a diversionary tactic, it is she who seeks to lead Jesus into a debate about religion. His prophetic insight into the condition of her soul has unnerved her, so once more she attempts to deflect his searching gaze. However, Jesus uses the opportunity to speak to her about the true nature of worship and how it can satisfy her thirsty soul.

We are all made to worship and everyone worships something. Sadly, when we do not know the living God, we end up worshipping false gods. For some, that may lead them into a literal form of idolatry and the worship of manmade images. For others, it may be expressed in the worship of money, fame, material possessions, career, sport and so on. There are many rivals to the love of God but none of them can satisfy the deepest longings of the human soul. All leave us dissatisfied, empty and, above all, thirsty.

Jesus reminds us that the true and living God is actually seeking for those who will worship him. Why is this? Partly, it is because as God he is deserving of our worship, and as his creatures it is right and proper that we should worship him and him alone. It is also for our sake, though, for when we worship, a special connection is made between ourselves and God that results in our sharing his life. As we worship and as we lift our hearts towards him, so his heart is opened towards us and his Spirit is poured into us afresh. Worship is one of the main ways by which we are able to drink the living water.

According to Jesus, those who want to worship God acceptably must worship him 'in spirit and in truth' (John 4:24). First, worship must arise from our hearts, from our innermost beings, or, to use the Bible term, our 'spirit'. This is the part of us that is made to commune with God. Before conversion, the human spirit is dead towards God but in regeneration it is made alive with the life of God (1 Corinthians 6:17). His Holy Spirit is joined with our human spirit and we become animated by the divine life within us. True worship flows not from the mind, the emotions or the will, but from our spirit. When we allow our spirit to worship God, we connect with the Holy Spirit in this same life-giving way, and we are refreshed and renewed even as we worship.

Second, acceptable worship must be offered 'in truth'. This means that it is a sincere and genuine expression of our heart. We mean what we say and what we sing. There is no place for pretence or formalism, hypocrisy or unreality. It also means that we are living out what we believe, as well as any of us are able to do. When God makes us aware of our sin, we respond with repentance. When he shows us his will, we seek to be obedient. There is integrity in the way that we live, congruence between our beliefs and our behaviours. This makes the worship connection with God alive and active so that the flow of his life towards us is uninterrupted.

Worship can therefore be compared to drinking. This is how THE MESSAGE puts it: 'Each of us is now a part of his resurrection body, refreshed and sustained at one fountain—his Spirit—where we all come to drink' (1 Corinthians 12:13). Worship should have a central place in our lives if we are to sustain ourselves in the long haul of ministry. We should take every opportunity possible to open our hearts to him in praise and thanksgiving, adoration and rejoicing, especially when we don't feel like it or when circumstances are against us. Then the discipline aspect of it comes to our aid. We choose to worship God. With the psalmist we say, 'I will extol the Lord at all times; his praise will always be on my lips' (Psalm 34:1).

When we see worship like this, we understand that where we worship is not as important as how we worship. The place is not what matters, whether it be Mount Gerizim (for the Samaritans) or Jerusalem (for the Jews). What counts is the attitude of our hearts. Further, when we worship is not as important as who we worship. We cannot worship in ignorance or hopefulness but must know God's salvation with assurance, in a personal way, and be able to call him Father.

It is natural that during our spiritual journey we have moments when we feel tired and weary. At such times it is important to stop and find spiritual refreshment. Jesus came to give us living water, and the well of salvation that he has dug for us is constantly available. Make sure that you not only slow down in the busyness of your life and work, but that you also take time to drink deeply of the water of life given to us so freely. Be a worshipper, in private and in public.

Reflection

- Consider the words of this hymn by Horatius Bonar (1808–1899). How does it speak to you?

  I heard the voice of Jesus say, 'Come unto me and rest;
  Lay down, thou weary one, lay down thy head upon my breast.'
  I came to Jesus as I was, weary and worn and sad;
  I found in him a resting place, and he has made me glad.

  I heard the voice of Jesus say, 'Behold, I freely give
  The living water; thirsty one, stoop down, and drink, and live.'
  I came to Jesus, and I drank of that life giving stream;
  My thirst was quenched, my soul revived, and now I live in him.

  I heard the voice of Jesus say, 'I am this dark world's light;
  Look unto me, thy morn shall rise, and all thy day be bright.'
  I looked to Jesus, and I found in him my star, my sun;
  And in that light of life I'll walk, till trav'lling days are done.

- How do you respond to the notion that the Christian life, from start to finish, is based upon grace? What might it mean to rest in grace as far as your own life and ministry are concerned? Read and meditate on 'The cycle of grace' in Appendix A of this book (p. 125).

- Think about worship as a spiritual discipline and also a way of connecting with the life of God. Why not spend some time worshipping or listening to worship music, as a response to this section of the book?

It's humbling to see God
at work on the journey

Working with God

Thus far in our exploration of working from a place of rest, we have been emphasising the importance of finding and establishing the place of rest within our lives. Once secured, this place becomes the springboard for our activity, which flows naturally out of our connectedness with God. We have taken time to lay this foundation of rest in God because it is so often lacking in our lives, and that is where we need to begin. But we are talking about *working* from a place of rest and we must now turn our attention to the way in which we operate in the new way of living that we have described.

Jesus is introduced to us in John 4 as a disciple maker—in fact, as a very successful disciple maker. His teaching is creating quite a stir and many are showing their allegiance to him by being baptised. The movement surrounding him is gaining momentum, greater than that which had surrounded even the ministry of John the Baptist, and the Pharisees are looking on with growing concern (vv. 1–2).

Disciple making is at the heart of Christian ministry and, however our service is expressed, it should always reflect at some point the desire to draw others into a personal relationship with God, so that they grow in their faith and set out on their own journey of discipleship. The ministry that Jesus began is to be continued by his Church (Matthew 28:16–20), so it is our work as well.

I have to say that, from the perspective of the church in Britain, it seems harder than ever to make disciples. In many parts of the world, the church is growing amazingly, but in the Western world it is not only stalled but shrinking. There seems to be little spiritual hunger around, and our best efforts produce very little.

We live in a climate of apathy in which the church is marginalised and considered irrelevant. In a context of religious pluralism and the relativism of a postmodern society, evangelism as traditionally practised can appear arrogant and confrontational and is generally unwelcome. Many of us feel the need to rethink how we share our faith with others. Watching how Jesus relates to the Samaritan woman fills me with hope that there is a better way to go about it. He models for us what I would call 'natural evangelism'. It is neither artificial nor forced but flows out of a vibrant relationship with God.

Notice the following points as we consider carefully how he went about the task of disciple making.

Being led by the Spirit

We noticed earlier the sense of inner conviction that made Jesus choose, on this occasion, to travel through Samaria on the way north, rather than skirt around it, as Jewish travellers often did. 'He must needs go through Samaria,' says the King James Bible, expressing the sense of divine necessity that prompted his decision. I think Jesus' conviction that this was the way to go was created in him by the Holy Spirit rather than by a decision to take the shortest route. Likewise, his choosing to stop by the well, rather than hurry onwards through this hostile territory, reflects his openness to the Spirit's prompting. Both are clear examples of his listening for the voice of the Father and being led by the Spirit in all he did.

If we are to be fruitful and effective in our ministries, it is imperative that we cultivate sensitivity to the voice of God and allow ourselves to be prompted by the Holy Spirit. We are promised that we will hear a voice behind us saying, 'This is the way; walk in it' (Isaiah 30:21) and, if we take the time to listen, we shall recognise the still, small voice of God within us. When we respond in obedience, we shall find ourselves directed to the places and people where God is already at work.

Sometimes we will have a very clear sense of the prompting of the Spirit, sometimes called 'divine breathings'—the gentle impressions we feel in our spirits, which we recognise as being from God. Richard Foster highlights the example of the Quaker John Woolman (1720–72), an itinerant preacher in the American colonies who campaigned against conscription, military taxation and, most importantly, slavery. A naturally shy and unassuming man, Woolman was not a confrontational person and was ahead of his time in his opposition to slavery. In his famous *Journals*, Woolman reveals how he cultivated receptiveness to the 'divine breathings', and how this prepared him to speak and act with courage when the time came. Foster notes:

Woolman steeped himself in the Presence of Divine Love and thus became increasingly familiar with its 'operations'... living in relationship to Divine Love, he increasingly took on its character... and increasingly formed by that character, he instinctively responded in ways that reflected Divine Love. He made decisions based upon what he had learned through relating with God.[30]

As we are led by the Spirit, we may not always be aware of any particular sensation. Sometimes it is a case of setting our sail to the wind of the Spirit and trusting that we will be led by God. At the start of the day we simply pray, 'Lord, lead me and guide me today' and trust that, as we move out into the activities of the day, God will indeed be guiding our steps. We do what seems right to do in the belief that he is guiding our choices. What is important is that we are seeking to live each day and each moment not according to our agenda but according to that which God has planned for us. If we take care to do this, we will often find ourselves in the right place at the right time, experiencing divine encounters as Jesus did at the well.

Having time to spare

We have noted already the importance of margin in our lives, especially when it comes to time. Jesus was able to develop a conversation with the woman because he had time to spare. He was sitting doing nothing—something most of us find very difficult. We suffer from what Henri Nouwen called the fear of the empty space: 'We are so concerned with being useful, effective, and in control that a useless, ineffective, and uncontrollable moment scares us and drives us right back to the security of having something valuable to do.'[31] Having little margin means that we have little time for the unexpected, and God is often in the unplanned moments of our lives. It means also that we have little time for people, passing them by in our hurry to get to our next appointment. We are like the religious professionals in the parable of the good Samaritan, rushing past on the other side with no time to stop and help (Luke 10:30–37). In our haste to do things for God, we may miss the real opportunities to do his will that come before us.

I know for myself that I live with a strong sense of purpose. When I am working at home, I sometimes go out to post letters at the end of the day. I march towards the post office purposefully and at a quick pace, living my purpose-driven life in which every second counts and it is important not to waste time. It used to be that a cursory 'Hello' was all I had to offer my neighbours as I accomplished yet another task in my well-ordered day—until God brought me up with a jolt and told me to slow down, enjoy the walk and, if I saw a neighbour, to stop and chat to them. Wasting time? It felt like it at first but I came to see it as an investment of time. How can I expect God to use me if I never have time to spare for the people around me? How can I get to know them if I have no time to be with them?

Developing an openness to people

What makes the encounter at the well possible is the amazing openness that Jesus shows towards the woman, who, from the start, is both hostile and defensive. There are several reasons why this conversation might never have taken place. First, as a rabbi and a man, Jesus was in danger of tarnishing his reputation by being alone with a woman, especially one of a doubtful reputation. Second, as a Jew, he ought not to have been associating with any Samaritan, since they were ritually impure and his own ceremonial purity might have been jeopardised by contact with her. Neither taboo seems to have bothered him. His attitude is one of openness, warmth and respect, and this sense of acceptance is somehow communicated to the woman through his manner and his words. A religious do-gooder with a holier-than-thou attitude is the last person she would want to meet, let alone have a conversation with, but somehow she is drawn to this man who is different from anyone she has ever met. He neither belittles nor condemns her, and, to her surprise, she feels safe in his presence.

I read recently that within 20 to 30 seconds of meeting someone new, we have summed them up and decided whether or not we like them. First impressions do count, don't they? God may look on the heart but we tend to notice outward appearance—a person's face, their hairstyle, the style of clothes they wear, how they speak, the colour of their skin, what car they drive, what their job is, their ethnicity, what their moral values appear to be, what religion they are, and so on. Even as Christians we can be guilty of prejudging people and making wrong assumptions about them. Sometimes racial prejudice can lurk in our hearts, and a lack of love can cut us off from individuals and groups who most need to hear our message.

In some of the crosscultural training I am involved in, the students have to read a famous article on missionary life called 'The world is too much with us' by anthropologist William Smalley. The article is about how we observe the people around us. Sometimes we see others merely as landscape: they fill in the background of our lives, like extras in a film, but we never really notice them. They are the passers-by, shadowy figures counting for little. Then we see others as machinery: they have a function to perform for us, like the checkout assistant, the parking attendant or the person who delivers the mail, but they remain faceless and nameless, valued only for the job they do. Only a few do we see as people whom we know, and with whom we have a relationship of love and trust.

This article really made me sit up and think about my own interactions with others. Do I notice them as people made by God and for God, whom he loves and wants to be part of his family? Do I treat everyone I meet with dignity and respect? Do I realise that God is at work in each and every life, and that perhaps he has a part for me to play in what he is doing? Smalley calls for a change of attitude, 'an intellectual and emotional conversion on our part to the point where we can become neighbours with all human beings everywhere'.[32]

Recognising the movements of God

A key element in working from a place of rest is to recognise when God is at work in a situation. This requires us to develop an internal awareness and recognition of divine activity. It is one thing to ask that God will lead and guide us but quite another to notice when he is opening up a conversation or creating an opportunity for us. If we pray this way, our responsibility is to be alert to what is going on around us and to seize the right moment. This kind of awareness is a learned skill: we become better at it, the more we practise it.

The conversation with the woman at the well develops not out of her asking for help (she is still unaware of her need) but because Jesus needs help. He is thirsty and wants a drink. It is his vulnerability and openness to receiving help that create the opening for a more meaningful conversation. We should not feel that we must always be the ones with the answers, or always the ones giving help; often, our weakness can be an opportunity. As we talk with people, though, we should be open to God so that he can show us when to nudge a conversation into spiritual matters. Again, it is about being aware of the working of the Holy Spirit and neither going ahead of him in our haste nor lagging behind him in our diffidence.

In my home church, we regularly pray that God will give us 'creative conversations'—that is, dialogues with other people in which it is easy and natural to talk about spiritual matters. It means that we must be friendly and outgoing, willing to overcome our natural reserve and ready to talk to whoever wants to talk to us. Then, as we talk, we can keep one ear tuned to the Spirit in case there is anything he wants to add to the conversation. This seems to be how Jesus developed his conversation with the Samaritan woman, and we could not have a better model to follow.

Going with the flow

How far we go in a conversation will depend on where the person is on their spiritual journey. Evangelism is a process, and the series of little steps that a person takes on their way to saving faith has been helpfully explained in the 'Engel Scale'.[33] This idea liberates us from the pressure to think that every conversation has to lead to a conversion. Sometimes it will, but more normally it will be part of the process that brings a person another step closer to Christ. If that happens, it has been effective and we can feel satisfied. Sensing how far to go in a conversation, and being respectful of how much someone can take, frees us from the kind of crass, insensitive evangelism that has given evangelicals such a bad name. It is also much more effective because it leaves the person in a positive frame of mind for the next conversation.

Jesus deals brilliantly with the Samaritan woman. He absorbs her initial hostility, refuses to be deflected by her denial of the reality of her personal situation, and avoids being diverted into a religious debate. Gently he probes and slowly he leads her deeper until she is really thinking for herself. All the time he is sensing her thirst for the living water, that here is a soul who is 'ripe' for harvest. Yet he is never heavyhanded or overbearing in his approach. Finally he helps her to that place where she can make her own confession: 'I know that Messiah is coming,' she says (v. 25). Then he leaves her with the great decision she has to make about his identity: 'I who speak to you am he' (v. 26). Now she must choose what to do next.

Give yourself to the opportunity

When God opens a door of opportunity, we have to go through it, however inconvenient that may be. All that took place in Sychar happened 'by accident' and that is the wonder of it. One commentator sums up the essence of what is really taking place: 'It is clear that Jesus did not leave Judaea with any fixed intention of ministering in Samaria, but the wind of the Spirit blows where it will, and the true messengers of God are never slaves to fixed programmes or pre-arranged plans of campaign.'[34] This was not 'Tell a Samaritan Week', or even an 'Every Home in Sychar' campaign! It came about because of the activity of God. The woman's testimony creates a stir in the nearby town and a crowd comes out to talk with Jesus. Now his peace is shattered and the quiet moment sitting by the well gone for ever, but that does not matter. Such is their spiritual hunger that the villagers beseech him to stay and teach them some more. It means an interruption to the schedule and a delay of two more days but, when there is a harvest to be reaped, who cares?

I was leading a retreat one summer at Penhurst in Sussex. The retreat house was situated in a tiny isolated hamlet with just three houses and an ancient church, ideal for those seeking quiet. After the morning session, one of the participants, June, went across to the church for her personal time of quiet. God often speaks to June through poetry, and that morning she wrote down what she felt he was saying to her and then left the church. Outside in the warm sunshine, she met two elderly gentlemen looking at the gravestones. Although she was meant to be in silence, June felt it would be all right to say a simple 'good morning' to them as she returned to the retreat house. However, the men were keen to talk and engaged her in conversation.

They explained that they often visited the church because it was so peaceful, and then one of the men began to pour out his heart about the troubles he was facing. As she listened, June realised that the words she had been given were not for herself but for the man. She explained what she had been doing in the church and asked if she could share the poem with him. He readily agreed and, as June read the words to him, tears began to stream down his cheeks. He was clearly touched by God. June said a simple prayer for them and then returned to join the rest of us, excited by the unexpected opportunity to witness.

Here she was, on a silent retreat in a remote Sussex hamlet, not meant to be talking to anyone and yet finding herself engaged in fruitful evangelism. Such encounters happen because it is exactly the way God works when we allow him—no effort, no strain, just being in the right place at the right time and being alert to what God is doing. That is what we mean by working from a place of rest.

14

The contemplative activist

The disciples return from their shopping trip to be greeted by two surprises. Throughout the three years that they were with Jesus, they were often slow on the uptake and did not always grasp what he was saying to them or understand the significance of his actions. Our attention turns to them now as they assess what has been happening during their absence, and as they are given some on-the-spot tuition in the ways of God.

Surprise number one is to find Jesus in conversation with a Samaritan woman. This clearly shocks them and they respond with embarrassed silence. No one asks the woman, 'What do you want?' or 'Can we help you?' None of them asks Jesus, 'Why are you talking with her?' (v. 27). They do not share his openness to people and cannot understand why he should demean himself by spending time with a despised Samaritan woman. They are still locked into the narrow-mindedness of their male, Jewish prejudice. It is one of their first lessons in the true nature of compassion and the wideness of God's mercy.

Surprise number two comes when, eventually, they gather their thoughts together sufficiently to urge Jesus to eat something. When they left him he had been tired, thirsty and hungry. Now they have brought supplies with them and they assume that he will want to eat—but no, he declines their offer of food. Moreover, he confuses them by saying, 'I have food to eat that you know nothing about' (v. 32). Can someone else have brought him food? Does he have a secret supply? Surely he is as hungry as they are? They are puzzled by the whole situation.

It is interesting to notice that Jesus spoke about living water to the woman and she misunderstood him, thinking he was referring to ordinary drinking water. Now he is talking to his disciples about spiritual food and they also misunderstand him, thinking only in literal, earthly ways. They appear unable, as yet, to see things from a spiritual perspective. He wants to open up their minds to a whole new way of thinking and being, but it is not going to be easy.

By way of explanation, Jesus makes this profound statement. 'My food is to do the will of him who sent me and to finish his work' (v. 34). In talking about food, he is really speaking about that which motivates and energises him most of all—the joy he finds in doing the Father's will. It is being about his Father's business that spurs him on, and it has been so since his childhood (Luke 2:49). Pleasing his heavenly Father and doing his will are his joy and delight (Hebrews 10:7); they are the reason he came into the world (John 6:38). So when he has the opportunity to speak with the Samaritan woman about eternal life, he is energised to such an extent that all thought of food vanishes from his mind. Spiritual reality sometimes takes precedence even over physical need.

Jesus was a hard worker, committed to accomplishing the task the Father had given to him: 'For the very work that the Father has given me to finish, and which I am doing, testifies that the Father has sent me' (John 5:36). Yes, he could rest; yes, he lived to the rhythm of the Sabbath day, and yes, he was willing to slip away from the crowds to be alone for a while, but he also knew how to labour. He didn't rush and he was never frantic, but there was an urgency about what he did: 'As long as it is day, we must do the work of him who sent me. Night is coming, when no one can work' (9:4). He was conscious of having a particular task to do but also of depending on the Father to carry it out. He lived in a conscious dependency, neither seeking his own agenda nor acting out of self-effort: 'The words I say to you are not just my own. Rather, it is the Father, living in me, who is doing his work' (14:10). He models for us exactly what it means to work from a place of rest.

For us, too, there is a time to rest and a time to work. In

establishing a place of rest in our lives, we do not want to run away from hard work; we want to provide a platform by which hard work can be sustained. We are not afraid to be busy, as long as our busyness has its origin in doing the Father's will and is generated by his life within us, not by self-effort or human zeal.

It is important that we integrate the contemplative strand (resting) with the activist strand (working) in our lives. It is not a question of separation, choosing one approach over the other. Nor is it a question of alternation, working hard and then collapsing in a heap. The activist strand is sustained and nourished by the contemplative one, and the contemplative strand finds its expression and outlet through the activist one. Writer and educationalist Parker Palmer puts it like this: 'Rather than speak of contemplation and action, we might speak of contemplation-and-action, letting the hyphens suggest what our language obscures: that the one cannot exist without the other.'[35] In this way we avoid the dangers and excesses of both, while benefiting from their strengths.

Palmer himself felt drawn to a contemplative lifestyle, being influenced greatly by the monastic ideals of Thomas Merton, but he soon discovered that he was not made to be a monk, becoming aware that he thrived most on the vitality and variety of the world of action. While being conscious of the dangers of activity for its own sake, he pleads for a spirituality that recognises the active life as having something good to offer. He feels that the contemporary emphasis on spirituality as essentially something inward devalues the God-given energy of those who, by nature, are more activist. 'The joys of action,' he says, 'are known to everyone who has done a job well, made something of beauty, given time and energy to a just cause.'[36]

Part of the rhythm of grace is to recognise the season of life that we are in. There are times of quiet and there are times of activity, and God will give us both. Harvest time is a particular season when we must be able to work hard, and it is about harvest that Jesus now speaks to his disciples. What he has to say re-emphasises that we must be willing to work hard in God's service but also that the work is his and we are called to labour, not alone but together with him.

It is not surprising that, with the background of an agrarian society, Jesus should use the metaphor of the harvest, which is found throughout the Bible. The first thing he says is that *the harvest is ready*. He quotes a popular proverb that said, 'Four months more and then the harvest' (v. 35)—the kind of saying that suggests, 'There's plenty of time, no need to rush'. Such a laid-back attitude can easily lead us to miss the opportunity of the moment. We need to be ready for action, not lazing around and dreaming of what is to come. The response of the woman and the approach of the townsfolk cause Jesus to remind his disciples that the harvest is ripe now. He is calling them to action.

The second thing to note is that *the harvest is people*. It may or may not be time to harvest the grain from the surrounding fields, but what is certain is that a Samaritan harvest awaits them. Some have said that the white (ripe) fields refer to the crowd of townsfolk approaching in their traditional white gowns. That may be so. It is clear, though, that Jesus is thinking of people receiving the gift of eternal life. This was why he came into the world, to seek and to save the lost, to gather into the kingdom all whom the Father was calling. In terms of their journey to faith, the townsfolk have reached a crucial moment of openness and responsiveness to the good news, so it is vital that the opportunity to teach and disciple them is taken up or it could be lost.

Third, *the harvest is teamwork*. Jesus mentions two categories of workers—those who sow and those who reap. Another proverb comes to mind, which this time he affirms as being true: while one sows, another does the reaping (v. 37). When harvest eventually comes, both can rejoice together and both can receive their reward. It is obviously important that we affirm both activities as being equally important. The sowers may not have much to show for their efforts immediately but without the sowing there can be no reaping. Some are called to sow the seed of the gospel, to bear witness as they are able, to begin the process that leads a person to faith. Others are reapers, given the privilege of helping others in the moment of conversion when the process reaches its climax. Whatever our calling, it is important that we play our part to the full but also acknowledge the contributions of others.

Finally, Jesus says that *the harvest is a gift*. We work hard for it but it still comes to us as a gift. This is true in the natural sense, for although the farmer prepares his ground and sows the seed, he is totally dependent upon God to send the rain that ensures a good crop (see, for example, Psalm 85:12; James 5:7). From a spiritual perspective, any harvest we enjoy is equally a gift of grace. In a short while, the disciples will be reaping what they have not worked for; others have done the backbreaking work of ploughing and sowing. Perhaps Jesus is referring here to Moses and the prophets, even John the Baptist. He could also be meaning himself or the prior work of the Holy Spirit. His point is obvious, though: the Samaritans are ready to believe because of someone else's labour. Those who will reap the harvest as they come to faith need to remember this and be humble, for their 'success' is the result of grace.

Paul confirms the idea that the harvest is based upon grace. Reflecting on his own ministry, he is aware that he can take no credit:

What, after all, is Apollos? And what is Paul? Only servants, through whom you came to believe—as the Lord has assigned to each his task. I planted the seed, Apollos watered it, but God made it grow. So neither he who plants nor he who waters is anything, but only God, who makes things grow. (1 Corinthians 3:5–7)

In the history of the Church worldwide, there have been many such moments of harvest when God has, in his sovereignty, drawn many people to himself at the same time. I share just one example that I am familiar with from the time when my wife and I were missionaries in Sarawak, Malaysia. The denomination we worked with there, the Sidang Injil Borneo (Evangelical Church of Borneo), traced its origins to the arrival in 1928 of a team of four young Australian men led by Hudson Southwell. They toiled in the north of the country without outward success for eleven years and then, at the outbreak of war in 1939, were interned by the Japanese in a prison camp in the southern town of Kuching.

During the time of imprisonment, they had no contact with the district where they had been working, but, from over the border in Indonesia, members of the Lun Bawang tribe arrived to share their newfound faith with their fellow tribespeople in the Malaysian jungles. When Hudson Southwell and two others were eventually released (one having died in the camp), they returned to the north to find people hungry to become Christians. Being a strongly communal society living in longhouses, the people wanted to convert not as individuals but as whole villages. Southwell recalled with us his joy and excitement as he travelled up and down the rivers, baptising hundreds as they came to Christ. He was given the nickname Tuan Sapu (Mr Sweeping Brush) by the local people because they said that he went up and down the country sweeping people into the kingdom.

The conversion of the Lun Bawang people, and other tribal groups, remains one of the most amazing people group movements anywhere in the world. It was definitely a case of the harvest being a gift. Those who did the reaping had done nothing to deserve the success they enjoyed. Others did the labour, and they reaped the benefits. It was God who gave the growth.

Those who understand what it means to work from a place of rest can well be described as 'contemplative activists'. They work just as hard as anyone else, yet they do so in a way that expresses their dependency on God and takes account of their own humanity. They are led rather than driven, and rested rather than rushed. They are partners with God in the great adventure of making disciples in all the world.

15

Nurturing new life

How do you cope with interruptions? For those of us who are task-focused and like to get as much done as we can in the time available, interruptions can be extremely irritating. Then, what about delays? When we are running to a tight schedule, anything that holds us back creates frustration within us, putting us under pressure and making us stressed. People who live with little or no margin in their lives inevitably experience high degrees of annoyance because life is always throwing up the unexpected and undermining our carefully laid plans.

While Jesus was very clear about the task in hand and totally committed to doing the Father's will, he does not seem to have fallen into the trap of being so tightly scheduled that he could not cope with interruptions and delays. The mini-revival that breaks out in Samaria was not planned and it presents an unexpected challenge to him. Now that spiritual hunger has been stirred in the hearts of the townsfolk, does he have time to stay and nurture them in their newfound faith? 'So when the Samaritans came to him, they urged him to stay with them, and he stayed two days' (v. 40).

From sitting leisurely by the well with time to spare, Jesus is suddenly thrust into a period of busy activity, a harvest moment that demands his full attention. Yet he remains unflustered and unconcerned by the disruption of his plans. He will be able to continue his journey to Galilee later. For now, establishing these new believers in their faith is his priority. This is the will of the Father for him in this moment and he embraces it gladly, responding with all the energy he has.

We can only wonder at the content of those two days of teaching.

We know that when he spent time with the two friends on the road to Emmaus, he gave them a crash course in the Old Testament and the fulfilment of prophecy, and his teaching touched them deeply (Luke 24:25–32). We can only imagine what the syllabus for this Samaritan retreat might have contained. Perhaps he explained more about eternal life and how the living water could satisfy their deepest longing. Maybe he spoke about the Father, helping them to a correct understanding of the nature of God. Possibly he taught them about worshipping God in spirit and in truth. We don't know how he began the work of discipling this spiritually hungry group. What we do know is that his words carried great power and that, for many more, it was the start of their discipleship journey: 'And because of his words many more became believers' (John 4:41).

We began our reflections on this story by thinking of the journey, and we end by considering the same theme but in relation to the woman and the townsfolk. It is the woman's testimony that is the catalyst for this movement of God, and her personal story is a remarkable example of the grace of God at work in someone's life. There is great power in sharing with others what God has done for us and explaining how he has changed us. People who know us can see the difference. This kind of living proof is more powerful than intellectual argument and cannot easily be denied. This woman was well known in the town, and not for good reasons. The change in her spoke eloquently of a power at work beyond herself and created a hunger in others for a similar encounter.

What state had she been in as she left the town that afternoon on her way to the well? We can only surmise, but she was probably alone, ostracised, something of a rebel and an outcast. There was a deadness inside her, for she had shut down all real emotion as a way of coping. We can see from her initial encounter with Jesus that she is extremely defensive. Her prickly responses give out a 'Don't come near' message. When the reality of her situation is exposed, she appears to be in denial: to take the spotlight away from her troubled soul, she tries a diversionary tactic, attempting to turn the conversation into a religious debate. All the while, though, her heart is softening and warming, and something is stirring deep inside. An awakening is taking place.

She has probably never considered herself a 'religious' type, but suddenly, as if from nowhere, a long-forgotten truth bursts into her consciousness. 'I know that Messiah is coming,' she blurts out (v. 25). It is probably a childhood memory and it catches her unawares. Then the words of Jesus cut right into her heart: 'I who speak to you am he' (v. 26). Now she can no longer stop the longing in her heart from rising up within her. She yearns for such a person—a Messiah, a Saviour, someone who will love and accept her for who she really is. Her mind is racing now and her heart is on fire. She knows that the man she is speaking to is that very person.

William Barclay comments on this moment: 'There are two revelations in Christianity; there is the revelation of God and the revelation of ourselves.'[37] The Samaritan woman has suddenly caught sight of herself in all her need, but it does not matter now for she has also caught sight of Jesus, the Messiah, the Saviour. The truth she could not face before, she can now accept, for here is mercy, forgiveness, acceptance and, above all, hope.

Even as she returns to the village, the transformation is continuing, carrying her from fear to faith, from doubt to assurance. 'Come, see a man who told me everything I ever did. Could this be the Christ?' she says to those she meets (v. 29). He is a man, yes, but more than a man. He is a prophet who can see right into your soul, but more than even a prophet. He must be the Christ we have been waiting for. He is here, in our town. You can meet him. I have found him.

The journey of the townsfolk is equally instructive. Few, if any, of them, would have woken that morning expecting their lives to be changed. The day would have begun like any other, full of the mundane, routine activities that make up ordinary lives. For many, spiritual hunger is deadened by low expectation. They have no sense of their own worth or value. They feel they are nobodies, almost invisible, just part of the crowd. How could God possibly be interested in them?

Their curiosity is aroused, however, by the woman's testimony. They know her and they know her lifestyle, and they don't care for either. But listening to her now, they can see that something dramatic has happened. Intrigued, they 'made their way towards him' (v. 30). What a beautiful expression that is, full of the deeper meaning so typical of John's writing! Their initial encounter with Jesus, plus the impact of the woman's testimony, creates faith in their hearts. It may be at a very basic level but it is faith none the less.

Their spiritual hunger having been aroused, they make a request to Jesus as a group. They want to know more, to be instructed further. Who will help them? So, as we have already seen, they ask an unusual and surprising favour of Jesus: 'they urged him to stay with them' (v. 40). Given the traditional hostility between Jews and Samaritans, this is itself a sign that something supernatural is happening. Just as incredible is the response of Jesus: '… and he stayed two days'. All barriers are broken down when the love of God is released and the Holy Spirit is at work.

We should not think, either, that this was an obvious or automatic response on the part of Jesus, as if it was something he felt obliged to do or could not refuse. Jesus would not allow himself to be 'bullied' into doing anything. He had the confidence to say 'No' if he sensed it was not the Father's will (see, for example, Luke 4:42–44 and Appendix B, p. 127). By contrast, we may find ourselves doing more than we should because we cannot say 'No', straying from our main focus because we allow other people and circumstances to dictate our agenda. Jesus stayed only because he knew it was the Father's will.

The time of intense instruction from Jesus causes the people's faith to grow even more. Not only do others believe for the first time but those who have already started to believe are confirmed in their faith. They turn to the Samaritan woman in excitement:

'We no longer believe just because of what you said; now we have heard for ourselves' (v. 42). They have moved from a somewhat second-hand faith, based on what happened to someone else, into a first-hand kind of belief where they know for themselves that it is true. It is a journey that many need to make, especially those brought up in Christian families or in strongly Christian contexts. We must embrace the truth for ourselves, not rest in the faith of those around us.

Before Jesus leaves, the Samaritan townsfolk take a final step forward in their faith journey. They begin to experience the truth not just in their heads but also in their hearts. They have their own moment of revelation, when the truth that they believe captivates them and they come to a deep assurance of faith. This kind of knowing is a spiritual knowing and is the work of the Holy Spirit: 'We know that this man really is the Saviour of the world' (v. 42). It is an amazing insight and a staggering claim for those so young in the faith. It would be many more months before the Twelve themselves would come to this level of revelation (Matthew 16:16)

This declaration of faith seems to be the signal for Jesus to move on and resume his own journey. The people have come to the point where their faith is established and it will take a lot to shake their newfound confidence, so Jesus is free to pursue the path that the Father has marked out for him: 'After the two days he left for Galilee' (v. 43). It is just as important to know when something has come to an end as it is to know when God is beginning a work. We need to let go of things as well as take hold of them. Although it would have been a sad parting, and the end of an amazing adventure, it is important for Jesus to keep in step with the Spirit, knowing that there will be other encounters ahead of him.

As I write this chapter, I am filled with a new optimism for what God can do through the lives of those who rest in him. These are wonderful examples of how God works in the lives of people to draw them to himself. The Father is still seeking worshippers, still longing for those he created to enjoy intimacy with himself.

The fields are still white for harvest, despite how the world may look from a human perspective, and there are men and women all around us, searching for that which we already possess. If we can develop the same openness to others that Jesus demonstrated, and if we can respond with obedience to the promptings of the Spirit, God can use us to introduce them to the one who is indeed the Saviour of the world.

Reflection

- How does the idea of 'natural evangelism' strike you? Which of the points made in this chapter seem to be most relevant to you?

- Why not try sitting on a park bench or in a shopping mall or the equivalent, and doing nothing for about 20 minutes? See if anyone comes and sits next to you. Let a conversation develop naturally and see where it leads you.

- Are you more drawn towards a contemplative approach or an activist one? What do you think are the strengths of the approach you naturally prefer, and what are its weaknesses? What would you need to do to become a 'contemplative activist'?

- How would you sum up the idea of 'working from a place of rest' to someone who had never heard of it?

✣

Conclusion

If you are reading this part of the book, it suggests that you have followed from the very beginning what I have been saying about working from a place of rest. It could be, of course, that you have simply opened the book randomly at this page, maybe as you browse through it wondering if it is worth buying. Then again, you might be reading this final chapter because you want to save yourself the hard work of reading the whole book! I hope the first scenario is true, because there is a development in what I am saying: the teaching builds up chapter by chapter and section by section. To make sure you have got the gist of what I am proposing, and to help you consolidate your thinking, I want to highlight the main points again.

We have taken this snapshot of Jesus sitting at Jacob's well, his conversation with the Samaritan woman, and his interaction with the people of Sychar, as a very practical and biblical example of what I have called 'working from a place of rest'. We have done so at length because it is my conviction that, if we are to avoid the dangers of burn-out and exhaustion, we must have a firm grasp of how we are meant to go about the task of Christian ministry. In reality, we often operate in human ways, conditioned by the world in which we live, rather than the ways of God. Therefore we may need to learn a different way altogether, one that takes its example from Jesus and not only sustains us over the long haul but makes us more effective as well.

Our first priority is to establish a place of rest. In the journey through life, with the demands of following Christ and being transformed into his likeness, it is natural that we become tired and weary. Jesus was tired, too, and that is why he sat by the well. His example gives us permission to stop in the midst of our own busy lives and be refreshed. By practising the discipline of stopping, developing a Sabbath way of living and taking time to be renewed through leisure, we can make sure we have some 'margin' in our lives and are not overwhelmed by the demands upon us.

Further, as we learn to slow down and to rest in God, we become more aware of his life within us. We become increasingly able to recognise when we are operating out of self-effort and human zeal, and can prayerfully choose instead to express our dependency upon God and allow him to work through us. We learn how to drink deeply of the water of life through the use of spiritual disciplines, to receive into ourselves the *zoe* life of God and the divine strength that is so readily available to us. The understanding that we have been invited into collaboration with God now grips us. We see life as a partnership in which he is always the senior partner and the initiator of all that we do. We can relax in what we do because the responsibility for the outcome lies not with us but with God.

This place of rest then becomes the launchpad for a life of active service. We are not less committed than other people but we do work in a different way. We watch for the signs that God is at work and respond to the nudges of the Spirit so that we are led by God in all we do. We live with a new openness to people, responding in faith and obedience whenever a door of opportunity opens to us. We work hard but not in our own strength. We have times of busyness and find ourselves stretched but always seek to remain centred upon God. We give ourselves unsparingly to other people but know how to take care of our own souls as well. Living in the rhythm of God's grace, we find that our lives are like the burning bush—on fire but not consumed.

Where does this leave you? What does God want you to do in response to what you have read? Are there changes he wants you to make in your lifestyle so that you can discover the place of rest? Does he want you to develop a greater sense of dependency upon him, a stronger realisation of the power at work within you as you work in collaboration with him? Is he inviting you to work *with* him, rather than *for* him?

Perhaps you are responsible for other people. Maybe you are a church leader with other paid staff under you and a group of willing volunteers around you. How can you create an ethos where people can learn to work from a place of rest? You could be the leader of a Christian organisation or mission agency, responsible for setting the direction and vision for the work. How will you care for those who are working for you? How can you develop an organisational culture that values both work and rest, and how can you model those values yourself?

I pray that, wherever you find yourself, you will be led to a closer relationship with God and to the continuing joy of working from a place of rest, where your life is centred on Jesus and his life is flowing through you to the blessing of others. And what I pray for you, I pray for myself.

⁜

Appendix A

The cycle of grace

There are several references throughout this book to the importance of understanding and experiencing God's grace. One of the most helpful ways of understanding how grace enables us to work from a place of rest is to be found in the idea of the Dynamic Cycle, developed by Frank Lake in his book *Clinical Theology* (originally published in 1996, revised and published by DLT, 1986). This is my own adaptation of his insights.

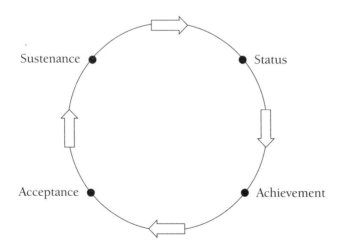

Following the example of Jesus, we derive our sense of acceptance from God, who created us and redeemed us and loves us unconditionally. We begin from the place of knowing that we are loved by God and start to live in a close relationship with him, finding our sustenance on a daily basis through our communion with him, drinking the living water that we have read about. Knowing that our worth is established in God, we can then begin to rest in our status as his beloved children and start discovering the unique calling he has for each of us. We can actively serve God out of this knowledge of who we really are: our achievement is the overflow of the life of God within us and an outworking of the relationship we have with him (collaboration). Any success we have is received humbly as a gift of grace. It brings us back to the place where we are reminded that our acceptance is because of God's grace towards us, not because of our accomplishments. The cycle then begins again. We are working from, or out of, a place of rest.

This is the ideal, of course, but we are all aware that sometimes we fall away from grace (Galatians 5:4) and try to find love, acceptance and worth through what we do. This causes us to go round the cycle in the opposite direction, and we end up trying to work ourselves into a place of rest. Not surprisingly, this leads only to frustration, exhaustion and burn-out.

When we allow this to happen, we strive for achievement in order to give ourselves a sense of status or worth. Having created a false sense of worth, derived from our own performance, we have to maintain it to keep hold of the feeling of well-being (sustenance), so that eventually we find the acceptance with God and others that we crave. This is really a precarious way to live, for we can never for a moment relax our effort or fail in our achievements without jeopardising our sense of worth. It leads us to being driven in the way we live and serve.

MY THANKS TO REVD NICK HELM (SPIRITUALITY ADVISOR FOR THE DIOCESE OF SHEFFIELD) FOR PERMISSION TO USE HIS VERSION OF THE DIAGRAM OF THE DYNAMIC CYCLE, TAKEN FROM HIS COURSE SOUL SPARK (WWW.SOULSPARK.ORG.UK).

✛

Appendix B

Times when Jesus said 'No'

We learn to say 'No' to some things so that we can say 'Yes' to God. 'No' is a freedom word because it liberates us from unnecessary and unproductive activities and helps us concentrate on our God-given calling. It is a boundary word, too, because it helps us (and others) to recognise our limits and prevents us from being overwhelmed by the needs and demands of others. We do not want to be negative or unhelpful, and nor do we wish to be restricted in the way we give ourselves to others, but we cannot do everything. A wise use of the word 'No' will save us from spending our energy on that which God has not asked us to do.

Consider these occasions when Jesus said 'no':

John 2:1–4	to his mother
John 7:1–6	to his brothers
Luke 10:40–42	to a close friend
Luke 8:38–39	to an enthusiastic follower
Matthew 20:20–23	to a strong personality
Matthew 12:38–39	to powerful critics
Luke 4:1–13	to Satan
Mark 14:35–36	to himself
Mark 8:31–33	to an easier way
Mark 1:36–38	to the demands of others
Mark 6:30–31	to busyness
Luke 4:42–44	to opportunity and need

John 6:14–15	to fame and power
Mark 11:11	to late nights
Mark 10:17–22	to flattery
Luke 4:16	to endless work

ADAPTED WITH PERMISSION FROM DR DEBBIE HAWKER

✢

Notes

1   Anslem Grun, *Jesus: the Image of Humanity* (Continuum, 2003), p. 79.

2   Henri Nouwen, *Jesus—A Gospel* (Orbis, 2001), p. 7.

3   Eugene Peterson, *A Long Obedience in the Same Direction* (IVP, 2000).

4   See *As You Like It*, Act II, Scene 7, where Shakespeare identifies the seven ages as infancy, schoolboy, lover, soldier, justice, pantaloon (old man) and second childhood.

5   Erik Erikson, *Childhood and Society* (W.W. Norton, 1963) (first published 1950).

6   Peter Feldmeier, *The Developing Christian* (Paulist Press, 2007); Janet Hagberg and Robert Guelich, *The Critical Journey* (Sheffield Publishing, 2005).

7   J.C. Ryle, *Expository Thoughts on John (Vol. 1)* (Banner of Truth, 1987), p. 199.

8   Louise Carpenter, article in *The Observer* (3 December 2006).

9   Richard Swenson, *Margin* (NavPress, 2004), p. 69.

10 Swenson, *Margin*, p. 56.

11 Swenson, *Margin*, p. 57.

12 I have been greatly helped in my thinking by David Kundtz, *Stopping* (Newleaf, 1998). My definition has evolved from that given by him on p. 14.

13 Marva J. Dawn, *The Sense of the Call* (Eerdmans, 2006), pp. 33, 35.

14 Marva J. Dawn, *Keeping the Sabbath Wholly* (Eerdmans, 1989).

15 Lynn Baab, *Sabbath Keeping* (IVP, 2005); Don Postema, *Catch your Breath* (Faith Alive, 1997); Wayne Muller, *Sabbath Rest* (Lion, 1999).

16 Robert Lee, 'Religion and leisure in American culture', *Theology Today*, Vol. 19, No. 1 (April 1962), p. 53.

17 Alan Richardson, *The Biblical Doctrine of Work* (SCM Press, 1952), p. 55.

18 Graham Neville, *Free Time* (University of Birmingham, 2004), p. 8.

19 Walter Rauschenbusch, *Christianizing the Social Order* (Macmillan, 1912), p. 248. Quoted by Robert Lee.

20 Ruth Fowke, *InterHealth Briefing Paper No. 5* (1997).

21 Stephen Cottrell, *Do Nothing to Change Your Life* (Church House Publishing, 2007), p. 5.

22 Cottrell, *Do Nothing*, pp. 12, 4.

23 Eugene Peterson, 'The pastor's Sabbath', *Leadership* (Spring 1985), p. 53.

24 Richard Foster, *Life with God* (Hodder & Stoughton, 2008), p. 166.

25 Foster, *Life with God*, p. 166.

26 Foster, *Life with God*, p. 198.

27 For further information and recent developments, see www.revealnow.com.

28 See my own book, *A Fruitful Life* (BRF, 2006), p. 73, for a discussion of the spiritual disciplines.

29 Dallas Willard, *The Great Omission* (Monarch, 2006), p. 61.

30 Foster, *Life with God*, p. 155.

31 Henri Nouwen, *Spiritual Direction* (Harper San Francisco, 2006), p. 18.

32 William A. Smalley, 'The world is too much with us', *Practical Anthropology*, Vol. 5, No. 5 (1958).

33 James F. Engel, *What's Gone Wrong with the Harvest?* (Zondervan, 1975).

34 R.V.G. Tasker, *Tyndale Commentary on John* (Tyndale Press, 1966), p. 75.

35 Parker J. Palmer, *The Active Life* (Jossey-Bass, 1990), p. 15.

36 Palmer, *Active Life*, p. 10.

37 William Barclay, *Commentary on John Vol. 1* (St Andrews Press, 1964), p. 149.

New Daylight

You may be interested to know that Tony Horsfall is a regular contributor to *New Daylight*, BRF's popular series of devotional Bible reading notes, edited by Naomi Starkey. Each issue covers four months of Bible reading and reflection, offering a daily Bible passage (text included), helpful comment and a prayer or meditation. *New Daylight* is also available in a Deluxe (large print) edition.

❏ I would like to take out a subscription myself (complete your name and address details only once)

❏ I would like to give a gift subscription (please complete both name and address sections below)

Your name _____

Your address _____

_____ Postcode _____

Tel _____ Email _____

Gift subscription name _____

Gift subscription address _____

_____ Postcode _____

Please send *New Daylight* beginning with the next January / May / September issue: (delete as applicable)

(please tick box)	UK	SURFACE	AIR MAIL
NEW DAYLIGHT	❏ £14.70	❏ £16.50	❏ £19.95
NEW DAYLIGHT DELUXE	❏ £18.00	❏ £23.10	❏ £29.55

(prices correct for May 2011 – January 2012)

Please complete the payment details below and send, with appropriate payment, to: **BRF, 15 The Chambers, Vineyard, Abingdon OX14 3FE.**

Total enclosed £ _____ (cheques should be made payable to 'BRF')

Please charge my Visa ❏ Mastercard ❏ Switch card ❏ with £ _____

Card number ☐☐☐☐☐☐☐☐☐☐☐☐☐☐☐☐☐☐☐

Expires ☐☐☐☐ **Security code** ☐☐☐ **Issue no (Switch only)** ☐☐☐☐

Signature (essential if paying by credit/Switch) _____

Also by Tony Horsfall

Mentoring for Spiritual Growth
Sharing the journey of faith

This book is an introduction to spiritual mentoring, for those who are exploring this aspect of discipleship or embarking on training for ministry as a mentor within their church. Over recent years the ancient Christian practice of spiritual direction has become increasingly popular, as more and more people from every part of the Church seek to know God more deeply. Terms such as 'mentoring' and 'soul' or 'spiritual friendship' are also being used to describe the process of one person coming alongside another to help them grow as a disciple of Jesus.

Tony Horsfall is an experienced spiritual mentor, and in this accessible book he explains through the metaphor of the journey both process and purpose—what mentoring means, its benefits to all involved, and how to explore the call to be a mentor to others. Written primarily for those unfamiliar with the whole area of spiritual direction, it will encourage you to prioritise your own spiritual growth as well as consider whether God may be calling you to be a 'soul friend'.

ISBN 978 1 84101 562 0   £7.99
Available from your local Christian bookshop or, in case of difficulty, direct from BRF using the order form on page 135.

Also from BRF

Time for Reflection
Meditations for use through the year

Ann Persson

It is not easy to switch from activity to stillness, from noise to silence, from achieving to letting go, from doing to being in the presence of God. This book of biblically rooted meditations provides accessible and practical routes to exploring prayer as that way of being in God's presence, letting the sediment of our lives settle so that we may have a true reflection of ourselves and of God within us.

Loosely based around the seasons of the Church year and also drawing inspiration from the seasons of nature, the meditations range from short 'spaces for grace' to longer exercises that can form the basis for a personal quiet day or retreat.

ISBN 978 1 84101 876 8   £8.99
Available from your local Christian bookshop or, in case of difficulty, direct from BRF using the order form on page 135.

ORDERFORM

REF	TITLE	PRICE	QTY	TOTAL
562 0	Mentoring for Spiritual Growth	£7.99		
876 8	Time for Reflection	£8.99		

POSTAGE AND PACKING CHARGES				
Order value	UK	Europe	Surface	Air Mail
£7.00 & under	£1.25	£3.00	£3.50	£5.50
£7.10–£30.00	£2.25	£5.50	£6.50	£10.00
Over £30.00	FREE	prices on request		

Postage and packing	
Donation	
TOTAL	

Name _____ Account Number _____

Address _____

_____ Postcode _____

Telephone Number_____

Email _____

Payment by: ❑ Cheque ❑ Mastercard ❑ Visa ❑ Postal Order ❑ Maestro

Card no ⬜⬜⬜⬜ ⬜⬜⬜⬜ ⬜⬜⬜⬜ ⬜⬜⬜⬜ ⬜⬜⬜

Valid from ⬜⬜⬜⬜ Expires ⬜⬜⬜⬜ Issue no. ⬜⬜⬜

Security code* ⬜⬜⬜ *Last 3 digits on the reverse of the card. Shaded boxes for
ESSENTIAL IN ORDER TO PROCESS YOUR ORDER Maestro use only

Signature _____ Date _____

All orders must be accompanied by the appropriate payment.

Please send your completed order form to:
BRF, 15 The Chambers, Vineyard, Abingdon OX14 3FE
Tel. 01865 319700 / Fax. 01865 319701 Email: enquiries@brf.org.uk

❑ Please send me further information about BRF publications.

Available from your local Christian bookshop.   BRF is a Registered Charity

About
brf:

BRF is a registered charity and also a limited company, and has been in existence since 1922. Through all that we do—producing resources, providing training, working face-to-face with adults and children, and via the web—we work to resource individuals and church communities in their Christian discipleship through the Bible, prayer and worship.

Our Barnabas children's team works with primary schools and churches to help children under 11, and the adults who work with them, to explore Christianity creatively and to bring the Bible alive.

To find out more about BRF and its core activities and ministries, visit:

www.brf.org.uk
www.brfonline.org.uk
www.barnabasinschools.org.uk
www.barnabasinchurches.org.uk
www.messychurch.org.uk
www.foundations21.org.uk

If you have any questions about BRF and our work, please email us at

enquiries@brf.org.uk